PRAISE FOR LUCY ELLMANN

'Lunatic and splenetic and distinctive... I begin to suspect [Lucy Ellmann] may be some sort of genius.' —*Telegraph*

'A true original.' —*Guardian*

'Ellmann's comedic brilliance is sui generis on any continent.' —*Paris Review*

'In a class of her own.' —*Cosmopolitan*

'If there were a laureate for anger, it should go to Lucy Ellmann.' —*Scotland on Sunday*

'A CAPITAL case of comic genius.' —*Independent*

'Funny, angry, sarcastic and utterly individual.' —*Observer*

PRAISE FOR *DUCKS, NEWBURYPORT*

WINNER OF THE 2019 GOLDSMITHS PRIZE · WINNER OF THE 2020 JAMES TAIT BLACK PRIZE FOR FICTION · SHORTLISTED FOR THE 2019 BOOKER PRIZE · SHORTLISTED FOR THE ORWELL PRIZE FOR POLITICAL FICTION · SHORTLISTED FOR THE SALTIRE PRIZE FOR FICTION

'That rare thing: a book which, not long after its publication, one can unhesitatingly call a masterpiece.' —Erica Wagner, chair of the judges, the Goldsmiths Prize

'The unstoppable monologue of an Ohio housewife in Lucy Ellmann's extraordinary *Ducks, Newburyport* is like nothing you've ever read before... Audacious and epic.' —2019 Booker Prize jury citation

'In her latest novel Lucy Ellmann doesn't just carry on as before: she doubles down, doubles up and absolutely goes for broke... Success? Failure? Triumph.' —Ian Samson, *Guardian*

'Resplendent in ambition, humour and humanity... In *Ducks, Newburyport* Ellmann has created a wisecracking, melancholy Mrs Dalloway for the internet age.' —Catherine Taylor, *Financial Times*

'A novel that rewards perseverance, is truly unique, and feels like an absence in your life when you finish it.' —Alex Preston, *Observer*

'Forbidding and magnificent... Ellmann has produced a domestic epic of modern American life in the Trump era.' —Arabella Byrne, *Prospect*

'Perhaps the most intensely real depiction of the life of the quotidian mind I've ever witnessed... [A] Joycean achievement... A colossal feat.' —Adam Smyth, *Spectator*

'What thrills is the novel's density, vibrancy and, crucially, its innovation... Turn to any page and you'll find it tightly packed and working overtime to redefine what the novel can do.' —Anna Leszkiewicz, *New Statesman*

'A feat of simultaneous compression and expansion... Among many other things, [*Ducks, Newburyport*] is a rebuke to the frequent downgrading of the "domestic" in literature.' —Alex Clark, *Guardian*

'Full of wit and intelligence... one of the most intriguing, charming and genuinely funny characters I have come across in recent years.' —Nick Major, *Herald*

'A bravura feat: a stream of consciousness, a transcript of the world under modern conditions, and (as a consequence of Ellmann's fierce and succinct wit) very funny.' —Rosemary Goring, *Scottish Review of Books*

'An impressive feat... Ellmann's 1024 pages put her male contemporaries in the shade.' —John Self, *Sunday Times*

'Astonishing... A Molly Bloom for middle America.' —*BBC Front Row*

'This amazing sustained narrative... may be the tour de force of our era, indeed "the great American novel" of now, arguably the greatest by a woman ever, or at the very least a masterpiece.' —Stoddard Martin, *Jewish Chronicle*

'Extraordinary... astounding... amazing... one of the outstanding books of the century, so far.' —Declan O'Driscoll, *Irish Times*

'The time and care that [Ellmann] lavishes on her narrator seem like their own form of political speculation — that every individual is owed an unending devotion, and that such devotion, applied universally, might change the fate of the world.' —Katy Waldman, *New Yorker*

'Ignore the laundry. Let this novel open like an oubliette under your feet.' —Parul Sehgal, *New York Times*

'Ellmann adeptly riffs on a vertiginous range of subjects... all the while carefully avoiding the didacticism that would warp the novel into either a soapbox or a gallows. Her heroine's anger burns cleanly, refusing the easy conflagration of self-righteousness. The cumulative effect is devastating. This is a powerful and deeply felt indictment of American moral failure, a fearful, dazzling bloom of conscience... A grand mimetic achievement.' —Dustin Illingworth, *Nation*

'A sublime literary enactment of how guilt, grief, rage, regret, compassion, and every other emotion swirls and ebbs in unbalanced defiance of rational logic... If art is measured by how skillfully it holds a mirror up to society, then Ellmann has surely written the most important novel of this era.' —Emma Garman, *Paris Review*

'Sei Shonagon [and] Walt Whitman... are the intellectual company Ellmann keeps... *Ducks, Newburyport* [is] as accumulative, as pointed, as death-addled, as joyous, as storied, as multitudinous and as large as life.' —Martin Riker, *New York Times*

'Timely, fresh... and possibly one of the most important books of the decade.' —Alexandra Marraccini, *Los Angeles Review of Books*

'Effervescent... Ellmann has made a case that a richer, less regimented language leads to a more vibrant and capacious mind, and has thus crafted the entrancing *Ducks, Newburyport* into a celebration of all that words, and the minds they build, can contain.' —Sebastian Sarti, *Chicago Review of Books*

THINGS
ARE
AGAINST US

THINGS
ARE
AGAINST US

Lucy Ellmann

GALLEY BEGGAR PRESS

First published in 2021 by Galley Beggar Press Limited
37 Dover Street, Norwich, NR2 3LG

Text design and typesetting by Tetragon, London
Set in Zuzana Licko's Filosofia, a 1996 Bodoni revival

Printed and bound by CPI Group (UK) Ltd, Croydon CR0 4YY

Sections of this book have previously appeared, in modified form, in various
publications. For a full list, please refer to the 'Sources' section at the end of the book.

A CIP catalogue record for this book is available from the British Library.

Papers used by Galley Beggar Press are from
well-managed forests and other responsible sources.

ISBN 978-1-913111-13-7

www.galleybeggar.co.uk

For Claire Lucido

All of life is pandemonium. With plague in our midst, every-thing feels like an emergency. I'm jittery, can't tolerate the least upset. So what else is new?

In times of pestilence, my fancy turns to shticks. They seem almost *innocent* to me, my scruples and my scorn, now that the whole human experiment seems to be drawing to a close.

Still, let's complain.

TABLE

OF DISCONTENTS

THINGS ARE
AGAINST US

You have to watch THINGS. THINGS are always making trouble, getting out of hand, trying to take advantage. THINGS do not have your best interests at heart. THINGS have their own agenda. THINGS care only for other THINGS. THINGS favour THINGS. THINGS indulge THINGS. THINGS prioritise THINGS. THINGS let THINGS get away with THINGS.

I speak as someone who is always losing THINGS, dropping THINGS, tripping over THINGS, breaking THINGS (even bits of my own body: bones, teeth, heart). Coming a cropper over THINGS. Okay, I'm accident-prone. But still, THINGS have a lot to answer for. The obstinacy, the indifference, the incorrigibility of THINGS! The recalcitrance of THINGS. So many disobedient and unbiddable THINGS. THINGS deceive you. THINGS perplex you. THINGS run out on you. THINGS look graspable when they aren't. THINGS slip out of your hand. THINGS look solid and steady when in fact they're wobbly: you step on the THING and you tip off.

Clothing rebels against the wearer. Socks won't stay up. Scarves are strangly THINGS. Hat brims blind you at crucial moments so you miss THINGS. Buttons try not to button THINGS. Pockets hide THINGS, or all too eagerly develop holes, defeating the whole purpose of a pocket, a THING designed to be a closed space with an opening at the top or maybe the side, but never the bottom. And who in hell invented the zipper? Like the atom bomb, not a good idea. Zippers can go badly wrong. Eventually, they *all* give out. Scary THINGS, zips.

THINGS disappoint us. Drawers stick so you can't get THINGS out of them or into them. Machines conk out. Rugs fade. Clothes shrink. Bookshelves fall on people; they are lethal THINGS. THINGS fall off hangers, and people fall off ladders. Ladders are dangerous THINGS. THINGS don't stay put. THINGS are never the right way up. THINGS get mouldy, THINGS break, THINGS drip, THINGS make odd noises, THINGS inexplicably collapse, THINGS move around in the night! THINGS get untidy. It is so hard to keep THINGS in order.

A kind of violence is done to us by THINGS all the time, unwieldy THINGS that awkwardly escape us, trick us, creep up on us. Soap slips from your grasp in the bath and you can't find it in the dark. The soap is dissolving while you splash around singeing your hair on the candle and getting water on the floor. All the tranquillity of bathing is upset by this dopey wrestling match. You catch hold of the soap briefly, then it slides away again! Giving up on the whole THING, you attempt to get out of the bath, a tricky THING at the best of times. Now you step on the slimy soap in the bottom of the tub, which causes you to slip. You grab the shower curtain, which tears right off its rail. You land on your slippery ass in the bathtub

and the momentum and curvature of the tub somehow com-
bine to propel you right out on to the floor, where you lie, all
wet and winded, seeing stars. This is a typical example of the
anarchy of THINGS. The enmity of THINGS. The conspiratorial
manoeuvrings of THINGS.

They may not always cause major calamities, but they suggest an underlying hostility. All I'm saying is that, if THINGS
can go wrong, they will. THINGS let us down. THINGS fail us.
Plumbing! What could be a more intimidating THING than that?
THINGS outwit you, THINGS flood your kitchen and then act
all innocent. THINGS pester you, THINGS try to bring you
down. And these various cumulative outrages committed by
THINGS are like little crimes against us, filling us with distrust
of the whole wide world, both the man-made THINGS and all
its other sweet parts. The unseen rock that jolts the foot, bird
shit on the head (odd that this doesn't happen *more*), three
buses at once...

Matches won't light – or else they explode, sending burning particles on to your hand or clothes or eyes. Fireworks are
notorious for boomeranging back onto the fuse-lighter. Rugs
grab you and knock you over whenever they can. Needles prick
you. They sit in the sewing box waiting patiently to prick you
some day. These THINGS never give up hope of a good prick.
Thimbles are merely an annoying collector's item, no help at
all. Use the wrong utensil when cooking spaghetti and you get
no end of trouble, a real show of resistance. The particular
pillowcase you wanted to find somehow manages to hide from
you, cleverly camouflaging itself amongst other pillowcases.
You thought you had THINGS sorted, huh? Once you find it,
the pillow tries every trick in the book to prevent itself being
inserted into the appointed pillowcase. Like a wild stallion, it

rears and leaps. Fitted sheets never fit. And duvet covers? Their deviltry is legendary.

THINGS fall into disarray – so fast! It's not fair. Pieces of paper frequently evade control: they either pile up threateningly, disappear unexpectedly, or give you a paper cut. They like to form themselves into unfathomable wads and cascading fans. They drift to the floor and you slip on them. Unopened envelopes are accusatory THINGS that emit unremitting waves of neglect and distrust.

You fill a hot-water bottle and then can't find the stopper THING. It has impishly hidden itself. When you finally spy it, cowering idiotically behind a bunch of dirty mugs, you reach for it with one hand, your other hand still holding the boiling hot hot-water bottle. The stopper now rolls off the counter on to the floor, clever THING. In your effort to retrieve the THING, you inevitably scald yourself.

Try dropping merely a small single piece of cardboard into the recycling bag. Will it go in with no trouble? Like hell it will. It always falls outside the recycling bag and goes straight down a crack in the floorboards. This is how we begin to realise THINGS are against us. In fact, it's possible THINGS really kind of hate us.

We all know about toast falling buttered side down. That is a cliché of the ill will of THINGS. But either way up the toast lands is not good! Why is it any better for it to fall butter side up? Okay, the floor might not get as greasy, and you won't have to mop all the butter up. But you've still got a dirty piece of toast on your hands, your buttery hands. Out it goes. Yeast has died for nothing. What a THING, what a THING.

THINGS get you coming and they get you going. THINGS go around and THINGS come around. When THINGS *can* mess with you, they will. THINGS are not shy. Some THINGS seem especially out to get you. Is it just clumsiness, or a jinx? You get out of bed on the wrong side and are at war with THINGS the rest of the day.

You try to cut up your salad and the choicest piece of lettuce falls to the floor.

The radish flies across the room.

You start the dishwasher, but then find a stray spoon.

When you open the dishwasher to place it carefully in the cutlery basket, the spoon falls to the side of the basket and ends up in the yucky murky detergent pond at the bottom of the dishwasher.

Out of fastidiousness or self-preservation, you naturally hesitate to delve into this swamp.

But you dutifully reach for the spoon anyway.

In bending over, your Kleenex, which was handily tucked in your armpit, replaces the spoon in the icky water.

Now your dishwasher has a soggy Kleenex in it and your sciatica's coming back.

It's so unseemly. So many stealthy attacks going on, cruel, cunning little acts of malice perpetrated upon us by THINGS. Some might say it's just not your day. I would say it's those pesky THINGS again. THINGS are out to get us.

Why do I always, always, pull the wrong cord on the blind, may I ask, making the darn THING go up instead of down, or vice versa? It's not just fifty per cent of the time that this happens, or even seventy-five per cent, it's *every time*. It isn't a nice THING about THINGS, that THINGS behave this way. It isn't kind. THINGS fall suspiciously often. THINGS are always testing us, testing, testing. Of course, gravity is an aid to THINGS in these plots and betrayals. THINGS take advantage of gravity

.too much. Gravity is helpless against THINGS. Centrifugal force is also a THING.

I guess I have a THING about THINGS. But why is it ovens get dirty so fast? Ovens do these THINGS to humiliate us. Why does jam get mouldy? Why do closets become impenetrable miasmas of junk? Why do people get locked out of their own houses? All the time! Of all the crazy THINGS. Keys are tricky THINGS. Why do the wheels break off your brand-new wheelie suitcase on its very first outing? Why do ankles get themselves sprained? Why so much dust and rust? THINGS are decaying all around us.

It is odd that we all own plastic feather dusters. What a strange THING to buy.

Then there's the way THINGS go missing. Those lost socks. Belligerent socks are racing to get away from us! Also pens, pencils, matches, hats, gloves, credit cards, and lemons (there are always fewer lemons lurking around the house than you thought). Is it because we just have too many THINGS in general, and THINGS feel crowded out, unwelcome? Do THINGS fear obsolescence? Surely that is their primary terror. If so, we must pity THINGS. It is the only THING to do.

If you have the right ingredients on hand when a THING goes missing, you can appeal to St Fanourious, saint of lost THINGS. You bake him a fanouropita out of a magical seven THINGS, or nine THINGS (always including lemon, flour, and sugar – this is why not having lemons at all times is a bad THING). Put the fanouropita by an open window. After invisibly partaking of the THING, St Fanourious will supposedly help you find whatever THING it is that you lost. Curiously, fanouriously, this cake remedy THING sometimes seems to work. But otherwise, all you can do is hope your lost THING miraculously appears again when the gods are feeling more forgiving about THINGS. Or when the THING itself relents. Because it's probably not the gods that are against us, but THINGS themselves.

A plastic takeaway container, used for storing dried thyme, falls to the floor as you rummage through your crazy mixed-up herbs and spices. It scatters little dried leaves of thyme every-where, just everywhere. These THINGS are on the floor, on the counter, in the dishwasher, probably in the bathtub. On every THING. Sharp little barely visible thyme leaves will keep turning up for centuries after your demise, accusingly tickling the feet of your descendants – all because you once dared do such a THING as rummage through the cupboard in search of some THING in there. Thyme leaves are extremely punitive THINGS.

Some people are more trusting of THINGS, and yes, I'm speaking here of my own dear husband, who will leave a glass of water, or the iPad, or our ancient dearly beloved salt bowl, right at the edge of a rickety table. I often find the teapot on the corner of the cutting board, giving it a vertiginous view of the three-foot drop below. Or pots are set to boil on the stovetop with their handles sticking straight *out*. The trusting fellow clearly has greater faith in THINGS than I have. In fact, he seems remarkably confident that he'll get away with these little dares without incurring the bad-tempered revenge of THINGS. Less convinced, I am forever shoving endangered THINGS inland from precipices about the place, and correcting the suicidal tendencies of THINGS. My position is, why take a chance on THINGS looking after themselves? THINGS are erratic, THINGS are unpredictable. THINGS are sometimes out-of-sorts. Lead THINGS not into temptation. You can lead THINGS to water but don't let them think.

What does it mean though, more profoundly, if all the innocent-looking THINGS in the world are actually determined to let us down? Because, if *inanimate* THINGS have it in for us, just think how much animosity *animate* THINGS must be feeling towards us – our contemporaries, I mean, the birds, the bees, giant killer hornets, snakes and snake-like THINGS. Spiders. This is why the hostility of THINGS is so unnerving. It rouses our fear of all kinds of other potential slights, carried out by stronger or sneakier THINGS.

How many thousands of tales of animal revenge are there? We unconsciously suspect animals will turn on us any minute. That would be bad enough. But what if *botanical* THINGS started acting up too? It would not be a nice THING to be attacked by a tree. (As lumberjacks well know.) And then there are all the poor vegetal THINGS which we are so used to bending to our will. Without a qualm, we grow these THINGS and pluck these THINGS and transport these THINGS and wash these THINGS and chop these THINGS and mash these THINGS and boil these THINGS and bake these THINGS and butter these THINGS and gobble them up. Or chomp their little heads off raw, poor THINGS! (Vegan recipes are often very complicated THINGS.) Any minute now, plants will turn out to be sentient THINGS, with all kinds of THINGS on their minds, and that'll give everybody a bit of a turn. Veggies will then feel as bad about THINGS as carnivores do. What if cauliflowers organised a walk-out sort of THING and leapt right out of your mouth, waving their pompoms? What if carrots objected to being grated, or were hurt by our laughter when they come out of the ground cross-legged, with a penis, apparently doing a jig?

A carrot, a cauliflower, and a radish go into a bar.

Barman says: 'What the hell do you guys want?'

The carrot replies: 'No crudités, please.'

We're all fully accustomed to the disobedience of computers. Those THINGS were sent to thwart us. But it's scarier to be attacked by familiar THINGS that supposedly belong to you and obey your will. Your tried and trusted toothbrush, a blanket, your own front door, or your phone wire, tangling itself up into a knot when you aren't looking.

And then, what a THING the *body* is. It works one day and not the next. Maybe it's okay for your first few decades or so (though even children get sick) but in old age it becomes a THING of terror. This is how most people end their days, finally succumbing to THINGS, including their own bodies. THINGS start taking it out on you. THINGS become useless, unreachable, untenable. THINGS like care homes are mooted. THINGS fly at you, THINGS block your path, THINGS drag you down. THINGS start to perplex you, escape you. Your dotage is a prime time for losing THINGS: you lose your way, your libido, your spectacles, your wits, your friends, your finances, muscle tone, and a lot of other THINGS besides. Your aim is off. You find it hard to navigate your way around. You forget which THING you went to the next room for. You forget the THINGS you were about to say. THINGS get you down. THINGS just don't go right.

THINGS start being against you, though, from *babyhood*. As an infant, THINGS are not in your favour. Hand-eye coordination is a difficult THING, and you have no control over your environment. You find THINGS bewildering. For newborns, THINGS are also out of focus. Being a baby is a pretty frustrating THING. This must be when you first begin to suspect that THINGS are shifty and unreliable. No wonder babies cry so much over every little THING.

We're probably best able to fend off the malevolence of THINGS in our twenties and thirties. At this point, many treacherous THINGS wait in abeyance, semi-contained, unable to take their full toll. But let your guard down even for a second, even in your prime, and THINGS will try to scupper you, no matter how resilient you think you are to THINGS. Your alarm clock will often disturb a good dream. At other times, its battery will die and you'll miss an appointment. The milk goes off. A water pipe will whine, or burst, and there's not a THING you can do about it. No matter how old you are, grapefruit will always spit in your eye. Those THINGS have an uncanny aim.

What better proof the spitefulness of THINGS than a viral pandemic? Viruses aren't even *alive*, in any sense that we can understand. They are just THINGS, THINGS which thrive on scuppering other THINGS. THINGS that long for chaos, THINGS that drive you crazy. Viruses want to bother us. They're bullying, troubling, thuggish THINGS, and their whole THING is to get us down. They are very determined little THINGS, and the THING they want to cause is disaster.

So THINGS, it must be said, are against us. But it's mutual. Humans are hostile to many THINGS, maybe even *most* THINGS. Our relationship with THINGS is discordant and haphazard. Our attitude to THINGS is intrinsically ungrateful. We're forever choosing this or that THING to be for, and ruling out a whole lot of other THINGS we don't like. Yes, we say, to sunsets; no to hurricanes. Yes to sunsets improved by hurricanes... Yes to cars, no to roadside weeds. Yes to pandas, no to mole rats. Yes to kittens, no to wolves. We've said no to wild THINGS till we're blue in the face – when *we're* the worst of them.

Are birds so bothered by THINGS? They don't seem it. When you're building a nest, stuff must go wrong all the time. No nails or glue available. If you drop THINGS, they land miles below. Twigs must sometimes refuse to be woven the way the bird planned. A cotton wool ball the bird carefully carried to the nest is whipped away by a breeze, an egg falls out, a cuckoo or cowbird baby is born. It's a tricky THING, at the best of times, bringing up young THINGS at a great height on a platter of grass in the crook of a tree branch. But birds soldier on, patient and forgiving towards THINGS. Birds just let THINGS be. Birds get on with THINGS. They don't dwell on THINGS, the usurpations committed against them by THINGS they can't control. Or I sure hope they don't, because it blights your life, having this THING about THINGS.

We bear grudges, and often take it out on THINGS: slamming doors, violently thwacking THINGS with a stick. We waste THINGS like water and plastic bags, and use up too much loo paper, just for the hell of it. We are mean to THINGS. We hurl THINGS when petulant, we squeeze THINGS harder than strictly necessary, we ignore THINGS, junk THINGS, fly-tip THINGS, refuse to clean or tend THINGS or repair THINGS or recycle THINGS. We disobey the clear will of THINGS. And with 3-D printers we even downgrade the organic integrity and traditional nature of THINGS!

All these little comebacks we have against THINGS – our revenge against THINGS for all the THINGS THINGS have dumped on us. And then, in the calm after the storm, we try to make THINGS up with THINGS, try to get along with THINGS again for a while if we can. But the rapprochement soon dissolves into some sort of sordid kind of stand-off THING, with each side doing little THINGS that eat away at bonhomie. THINGS have their own agenda, and it's rarely our kind of THING.

THINGS probably started it, but we've carried on the fight: polluting THINGS, shooting THINGS, refuting the basic nature of THINGS. Lugging poor old boulders all the way to Stonehenge... We're always wrecking THINGS, exploiting THINGS, belittling THINGS, dislodging THINGS, exacerbating THINGS, delaying THINGS, extinguishing THINGS. We are so ignorant of THINGS. We just don't fit into the grand scheme of THINGS, and THINGS know it.

So it's understandable THINGS might take the hump.

THE UNDERGROUND
BUNKER

On January 6, 2021, the USA imploded. Trump's rabid follow-
ers, a lynch mob sporting Nazi slogans, nooses, Confederate
flags, guns, spears, explosives, and plastic zip-tie handcuffs,
attempted a coup. They rioted, assaulted police and reporters,
broke into offices and scared politicians half to death with the
threat of assassination. They erected a gallows outside the Capitol
building, sprayed gas at opponents, and desecrated a public
landmark with pee and shit and blood and spit. They killed one
police officer by beating him with flags and a fire extinguisher.
With others they took selfies. To cap it off, they participated in
a superspreader event during a pandemic. All because their
leader, a delusional mass murderer (who let thousands die from
Covid-19) wanted to continue illegally as president. And what a
president. The MAGA hats and Trump brand are now signs of
infamy. But those treasonous bums had the time of their lives!

Still, Americans blather on about how great America is. They'll salute their ruined nation till the whole place is awash in corpses, swastikas, and radioactive waste. They'll be clinging to the roof, barbecuing steaks up there, talking god and cars and UFOs and QVC jewellery lines until there's nothing left alive but a few DDT-resistant bugs.

Americans are acutely unaware of the past and the future. Also, the present. History is infinitely malleable for them. So is reality. Are they just undereducated, indoctrinated, chronically indifferent, hypnotised, or too damn busy makin' a buck? Consumed by consumerism, they wallow in army fatigues and self-regard, coveting the next dynamite Apple doodad or an AK-47, plasma screen and some Nikes. They have worried everybody and *ruined the earth*, all so that they can prance around, effect insouciance, drink beer, watch football, guzzle Sloppy Joes and Oreos, wear pro-Auschwitz sweatshirts, make pipe bombs, absorb incessant rock music, object to positive discrimination and the public display of female nipples, wonder whether the mailman has shut the mailbox properly, and choose a new euphemism for excretion yearly.

Dazed and furious, they wrestle with a world of distraction and fake facts, their minds ravaged by malign corporations, PFAs, PCBs, dioxins, cocaine, caffeine, and any creed on offer – American god-lust is among the many forms of self-sabotage that gave us this male-order muppet show in the first place. The US is now the worst Boy Scout jamboree or jerk circle in history.

MEN HAVE GLORIED IN THIS. Men with their hierarchies, their secret handshakes, gang warfare, ownership, privilege, entitlement, and extra helpings of roasted meat. They glory in death, and the chastening of women. Women are exhausted!

Fifty women a day are shot dead in America by so-called partners. How can women thrive in such a society?

Not just in America but elsewhere too. What have we got to
show for putting up with thousands of years of male rule? On
the plus side, Roman mosaics, rocking chairs, and the Chrysler
Building. On the minus? Fascism, poverty, carnage, the Large
Hadron Collider, tornadoes, tirades, Boogaloo Bois, Three
Percenters, Elk reunions, the internal combustion engine, and
oceanic levels of plastic.

Patriarchy has trashed the place. Wildlife is pretty much
finished now. Walruses drop helplessly to their deaths from
iceless rocks. Soon there will be no orangutans. There are now
queues on Mount Everest. Next thing you know, everyone will
insist on riding the Loch Ness monster.

Men have wrecked everything of beauty and cultivated everything putrid on the face of the earth. Not *all* men, of course,
yeah, yeah, yeah, I know I'm generalising. But it's for a good
cause: sanity. Men have a death wish. Violence is not just a drug
for them, it's a security blanket.

Men learn early on to mock the female body. Girls are mocked
for *menstruating*, which they cannot help, and breastfeeding too
is frowned on by many a well-fed man. Everything women do
is taboo. Anything men can do, women can do better – but
somehow, everything women do, men say *stinks*.

Men couldn't oppress us any better if they really did get
together in an underground bunker and plan the whole thing
out. Which I half-suspect they do. How else would they all come
up with the same identical thoughts on high heels, inflatable
sex dolls, and the pay gap? (Though Trump's taste in femininity
always seemed a little corny.) In the absence of anything positive
to contribute, male power rests on a tiresome combination of

volition, violation, and volatility, along with booze, biz, bellowing, and boring the pants off you.

The United States of America has now reached a whole new level of patriarchal absurdity. You mean they massacred the Indians, enslaved the Africans, cut down all the trees, poisoned all the rivers, and extinguished or imprisoned all the animals for THIS, this hellhole of bombast and hamburgers and opioid addictions and cardboard-box houses and pretend ideas? You mean they used up all the oxygen on 4th of July firecrackers and forcing kids to pledge allegiance to the flag every goddam day, drank Coke till they choked, spat tobaccy till they puked, fought cancer (but only for people with lots of money), nestled in Nestlés, slurped slurpees, burped burpees, handed on herpes, Tasered the wayward, jailed the frail and tortured about a million billion chickens (then fried and ate them), just so people can drive around and shoot each other and create GoFundMe sites to pay the hospital bills?

Make America abate again.

TRAPPED
FAMILY FINGERS

When exactly did America give up on love of life? Are they the victims of some awful *experiment*? You almost expect the gigantic bald pate of a mad scientist to appear over the Rockies one day, checking on his helpless specimens, all stuck in their hamster wheels of indefatigable optimism.

Flummoxed by fake facts, Fox News, and the phoniest guy they could find for prez,[1] Americans rely on Disney for comfort, along with vaccine evasion, Vietnam bombing-raid re-enactments, and whole days devoted to YouTube gaming videos. For the few remaining centrists and liberals, there's a self-congratulatory movie now and then about Ruth Bader Ginsberg or the more prominent heroes of the Underground Railway — while everyone

---

[1] NB. This essay was originally written when the Trump regime was in full flower. Luckily, everything's fine now — apart from the lingering presence of guns, war, racism, sexism, fundamentalism, terrorism, democracy defilers, tornadoes, hurricanes, wildfires, forever chemicals, universal cerebral underdevelopment, and wretched TV series.

unites to await execution at church, the mall, the gas station, convenience store, or parking lot. Or, of course, at home.

When they tire of killing *each other*, they slaughter some Iraqis or Afghans. No wonder extraterrestrials haven't the stomach to visit the US any more.

Every child in America has now been drilled in how to climb under the desk when a shooting spree is going on. The latest idea for preventing school shootings is to train *dogs* to confront the gunman. The dog is supposed to make his or her way to the homicidal maniac, mid-rampage, and wrestle him to the ground. These are kamikaze K-9s, doomed from the start to be shot along with everybody else.

Or here's a good move: arm the teachers! This they've done and, as a result, children are now exposed to guns, gun threats, and gun accidents at school every day. Parents dutifully join campaigns for 'gun sense' while their kids have nightmares and panic attacks and try to run faster than a speeding bullet.

For extra protection (at least for the upper torso, if shot from the rear), your child can wear a bulletproof backpack:

THREE TIMES THE FUN!

BOOK BAG, LUNCH PAIL AND LIFE-PRESERVER, ALL IN ONE!

Or just pretend Sandy Hook and Parkland never actually happened. Then you don't have to doubt the American system at all.

Never in all this is the possibility of simply *banning all firearms* raised. Forget gun *control*, gun reform, gun sense. How about NO GUNS? There is no unassailable right to own a gun or be shot. Babies are not yet born armed.

But not to worry. Rube Goldberg's here and he's just turned on his think-faucet! Republican senator (A), on way to receive large cash donation (B) from NRA (C), slips on wife's alligator handbag (D), out of which flies cockatoo (E). While senator is out cold, bird spies blueberry muffin (F) on desk (G) and settles in for big breakfast. Scrabbling about, cockatoo upsets bottle of Kahlúa (H). Bottle spills, bird steps in puddle (I), and produces sloppy but legally 'X' on important document banning guns (J), which only required one more signature. Before senator (A) even regains consciousness, total ban on private ownership of guns in America has been instituted, and all guns (K) have been thrown into either Pacific (L) or Atlantic (M). Random child (N) is now able to attend random elementary school (O) in safety and learn alphabet (PQRSTUVWXYZ).

～

Freud said America was a big mistake, presumably because it was a place where the id was allowed to run rampant, from Columbus's outrages on through all the land-grabbing, massacres, slavery, greed, insensibility, Oscars ceremonies, and ice-cream sundaes. As Randy Newman put it:

> *Hide your wives and daughters, hide your groceries too,*
> *Great nations of Europe coming through.*

By the mid-1800s, the experiment had undeniably turned sour. Fanny Trollope was *appalled* by Americans, finding them not only cheerless, misogynistic, murderous, and unneighbourly, but so vulgar! They ate with their knives and she couldn't believe how much they spat. The only time they seemed to brighten up a bit was on Independence Day, or at least the *men* did ('women have but little to do with the pageantry, the splendour, or the gaiety of the day', she wrote):

> On the 4th of July the hearts of the people seem to awaken from a three hundred and sixty-four days' sleep; they appear high-spirited, gay, animated, social, generous, or at least liberal in expense; and would they but refrain from spitting on that hallowed day, I should say, that on the 4th of July, at least, they appeared to be an amiable people.[2]

Some spit, others are spat out. The go-getters go get, the rest get got. The US has long teetered on the verge of 'mobology' and is subject to the 'mobocratic spirit', as Lincoln put it.[3] America was always each man for himself, with a big investment in lawlessness. Abolition's still a work in progress.

Carlos Fuentes identified the 'anguish' intrinsic to the American way of life, the anguish of 'doing, getting things done, making it'. Failure, pretty much guaranteed in such a merciless set-up, goes unloved. That's why Trump, one of the biggest failures of all time, tried to transmogrify his every fiasco into a supposed success.

Fear of failure drives Americans into uptight bubbles of ME, only relieved by the collective daily orgasm of consumerism. Shopping is proof of citizenship. This provides Americans with the *us* in US. (Undocumented 'Dreamers' just dream of buying stuff.)

Even the *niceness* of many Americans seems suspect, because you never know if it's just a precautionary kindness. What if all

---

2 *Domestic Manners of the Americans* (1832).
3 See Philip Gourevitch's remarkably prescient 'Abraham Lincoln Warned Us About Donald Trump' (*New Yorker*, March 15, 2016).

those chocolate chip cookies suburbanites offer each other are really SOS messages? Chip-on-the-shoulder cookies. What if American politeness stems from Stockholm syndrome: three hundred and thirty million captives, all being pleasant just to avoid being shot in the head?

'When terror descends' (as Edward Albee put it[4]), these helpless, cornered creatures easily swap democratic rights for gossip, lobbyists, peer pressure, Super PACs, gerrymandering, voting restrictions, that antique gewgaw the Electoral College, pre-election dismantling of the postal service and post-election dismantling of the vote count.

'I just want to find eleven thousand, seven hundred and eighty votes,' Trump boldly declared, two whole months after losing the 2020 election. Sad.

But there's an upside! All this powerlessness leaves more time for the ME stuff. Because, you know, there's like all this pop music to consider, cosmetics to apply, and foreign slave-labour jeans to purchase, so many beggars to belittle, billionaires to emulate, elders to ignore, and theories about the purifying effects of mindfulness or green tea to propound. So much purifying and putrefying going on. It's really very absorbing! Never mind what the police are doing just down the street to Black men who don't mow their lawns in the right direction.

∿

Patriotism, charity, and heroism have been replaced by one essential task: the moral duty to go to the gym. If only these people, so enamoured of exercise, would use their muscles for

---

4 *A Delicate Balance* (1966).

the greater good. Instead of scolding the sedentary, these eager beavers could help out a bit more. Plant trees, lug food to the poor, scoop plastic crap out of rivers, fortify cities against flood and fire. Forfeit their cars and run (if run they must) to work. *March* too, on Washington – and *stay there*, dammit, till all the nitwits depart.

But so much time is devoted to the self, there's none left for society. Americans count the calories, not the capitalists. Meanwhile, the ICE man cometh: Guantanamo wasn't enough for everybody, the Republicans now want *immigrants* incarcerated for life too.

At the sight of child prisons and all the screaming, self-described liberals cry out, 'This is not America, this is not who we are!' But it so clearly *is* who they are. Or what they became while drinking the requisite amount of sody-pop and gawping at their smartphones.

'Why can't I have anything just for me? Is that so selfish?'
'Actually, that's the definition of selfish.'[5]

Americans hardly think beyond the bounds of family. Thanksgiving and Xmas won out against the Covid scare. These are people drowning in family life, family fun, family businesses, family secrets, Family Paks of aspirin and burger buns, Family Size gallons of milk, beer, and OJ (the drink, not the felon), family cars big enough to shove trucks off the road, family pets, family movies, family vacations, family affiliations, family trees, family traits, family genetic diseases, family men, family matters, family favourites, family hunting trips, family vendettas, family murder–suicides.

---

5 A George and Jerry debate in *Seinfeld*.

Americans are trapped in trapped families – and the hills are alive with the sound of gunfire.

You'd think *mothers* might be awarded high status in such a family-oriented set-up, but women in America have no status at all. As we saw with the Brett Kavanaugh hearings, not only are some men called *Brett*, but American women never get a word in edgewise.

Professor Christine Blasey Ford offered the nation a lesson on integrity. It didn't take.[6] The US is really just one big internment camp for women, where they are gagged, cuffed, and detained, awaiting a (fair) hearing.

> *Kavanaugh good for Amer-ic-a.*
> *Women not heard in Amer-ic-a.*
> *Women not safe in Amer-ic-a.*
> *Women just slaves in Amer-ic-a,*
> *free to wait tables and shine shoes.*

America's no place for women. It's so depraved that a woman can't even work a shit job in a shirt store without having to choose one day if she wants to be sodomised or shot in the head. Whatever happened to compassion, or a sense of community? But *that* word is awkwardly close in sound to *communism*, which frightens Americans more than death itself. (And the intensity of that fear frightens everybody else!) All their help-thy-neighbour impulses quail at the mere hint of communism. Socialism too – though paradoxically they don't

---

6 She bravely testified to a Senate Judiciary Committee that Kavanaugh had sexually assaulted her when they were teenagers, and laughed at her. But Kavanaugh still won his place on the Supreme Court (though by just two votes, the smallest margin for a hundred and forty years).

mind socialist programmes like Medicare, state education, the fire service, search and rescue volunteers, national parks, and transport infrastructure. The latest nickname for protestors against climate change, people hoping to *preserve future life on earth*, is 'watermelons': green on the outside and red on the inside.

Nah, we don't want life on earth. Leave us alone.

⌐∿

Just as Brexit is the apotheosis of age-old British self-hatred, America embarked in 2016 on its own act of self-immolation. The nation mulled things over, Stan Laurel-style, blinked its eyes, scratched its head, and decided to go for *more* corporate criminality, *more* exploitation, *more* inequity, *more* poverty, *more* sickness, *more* indifference, *more* conformism, *more* conservativism, *more* waste, *more* plastic, *more* violence. And astonishing levels of sadness. The mad scientist must be about to begin his vivisection. Obediently, the lab rats lounge before their big TV screens, munching apocalypse stew – dumbo gumbo – and railing against RINOs,[7] every house blazing with the sinister blue light of unreason.

What riches there once were, what beauties! Raindrops on roses and crop tops on cuties. Now it's just tear gas and water hoses, and Mexican children tied up with strings. *These* are a few of their favourite things. Quarry every mountain, wreck every stream.

---

7 Republican In Name Only: hated by fascist, white-supremacist Republicans; liked by over-optimistic Democrats.

Sure thing, ma'am, long as it's worth frackin'.

But wait! It's Rube again to the rescue! New president (A) clips previous president (B) on ass (C) with old boot (D) and makes reparations to Native Americans (E), African Americans (F), women (G), alligators (H), and oil-caked sea otters (I). He then reinstates US Constitution (J), establishes universal Medicare (K), defunds the police (L), distributes basic living wage to every citizen (M), bans guns (N), saves whales (O), opens all borders (P), dismantles nuclear plants (Q), discards nuclear weapons and weapons deals (R), undermines power of big tech companies (S), establishes Green New Deal (T), and erases student debt (U). What's more, he delightedly extracts Trump's back taxes (V) and catapults resultant dough into education (W), so scariest nation on earth (X) won't fall into drainage canal (Y) of vapidity (Z) ever again.

Wow, what a relief. I thought we were all goners.[8]

---

8 There may be hope yet for America: on January 15, 2021, the NRA went bankrupt.

THREE STRIKES[1]

I made nice.[2] It didn't work. Women are still oppressed, men still running the show, still running around raping, killing, and maiming women – raping, killing, and maiming *children* too

---

1 In baseball, three strikes and you're out. Out on your ass. The expression therefore has some bearing on the trajectory of this essay, my pitch being that men are swinging wild. The original idea for the piece came from reading Virginia Woolf's *Three Guineas* (Hogarth Press, 1938), to which I was alerted by a friend, the novelist Peter Burnett. But I couldn't refer to three letters, as Woolf does, since nobody *writes* letters any more; and I chose strikes to replace her guineas, since nobody knows what a *guinea* is any more either. Woolf is being ironic about money anyway. With eccentric thoroughness and wit, her essay considers various good causes to which three guineas could usefully be put: the prevention of war; rebuilding a women's college in Cambridge; or finding employment for women in the professions. She finally offers a guinea to each cause, this being all an 'educated gentleman's daughter' could afford. Woolf's three guineas thus become, in their paltriness, both a significant gesture in the right direction and an emblem of women's second-class status. The limitations imposed on women are the real subject of Woolf's essay. But there's something tenacious about the image of those three guineas. They can't be denied. It may be hard now to imagine behaving patronisingly towards Virginia Woolf – aren't we all supposed to be *afraid* of her? – but she was well aware of what both the 'intelligentsia and ignorantsia' put women through. In *Three Guineas*, she concludes that women are outsiders – but in a good way. So are the many footnotes in Woolf's essay. Footnotes are the outsiders within a text, and make obliging underdogs in an essay on female subordination.

2 As George Bernard Shaw said on his second arrival in America, 'I told you what to do and you haven't done it.' I put my solution to male violence towards women in the most palatable form I could think up, a romcom novel called *Mimi* (Bloomsbury, 2013) about a rich guy in New York who sees the light and becomes a champion of women. *Mimi*'s solution to the downward spiral of patriarchal insanity is: *hand over the money*. Transfer all wealth into female control. Not *half* of it, not fifty-two per cent either – ALL THE MONEY. Given the mean little way late capitalism works, a steady wholesale redistribution of wealth seems the simplest method of ensuring women get respected more, and raped and murdered less (femicidal violence being a five-thousand-year-old fad, embedded in women's low social status). Until we can return to a matriarchal form of socialism (or 'commonism', as another friend, the novelist John Aberdein, puts it) in which money has *no place*, we must in the short term put women in possession of serious wealth. This pro-female asset-reset, which in *Mimi* I dubbed the Odalisque Revolution, would be a peaceful form of male revolt – yes, it's *men* who will need to do the work here, if they want to join the Odalisque Revolution (women are automatic members). It could be progressed on an *individual* basis, in private, by any right-thinking man who's tired of hearing about women being deprived, denied, doubted, despised, derided, deluded, defamed, ignored, cheated, exploited, blamed, vilified, cajoled, threatened, violated, killed, overworked, messed with, ordered about, and ground into the dirt. It's not just about *money* though. The ultimate aim of the Odalisque Revolution is to start a new matriarchal era. Such a revolution seems to me a safe, sensible, efficient, and really rather innocuous solution to the devastation caused by male mayhem and wars and depredations of the environment. And yet hardly any men to my knowledge have followed my very clear instructions on how they can relinquish the unfair advantages so many claim to abhor. Only one person (the intrepid writer and critic Anthony Rudolf) has actually asked to have his Odalisque Revolution Mea Culpa Declaration stamped. The detachable certificate, once stamped, ensures membership of the Odalisque Revolution. It can be found at the back of any copy of *Mimi*, and all the contrite philogynist has to do is sign it and give everything he's got (or *most* of it: he can keep some petty cash, for pizza's sake) to a woman, or women, of his choice. The Declaration (see footnote 59), written in plain English, invites the signatory to admit that male property and power are ill-gotten gains, the products of men's ancient and misguided terrorist campaign aimed at the usurpation of women and, to redress this, the signatory pledges to hand over all his assets to women. Strangely enough, few besides my dear husband Todd McEwen have shown any sign of wholly acquiescing to my demands. No one has even asked me to defend my position. Instead, the usual male silence: the unspoken policy seems to be to deprive my wealth-redistribution idea of oxygen by not responding to it at all. Even some *female* reviewers surfaced to voice doubts, flinging around examples of unworthy female leaders such as Margaret Thatcher, Elizabeth I, and Lady Macbeth. Now, wait a minute! You're

41

(another way of attacking women). They're still waging war, spraying every living thing with pesticide, distributing micro-particles of plastic everywhere, eating huge pizzas,[3] and charging an awful lot for a haircut, highlights, and blow-dry. Or how about this new craze for murder-suicide, that apparently culpritless crime, whereby the execution of women and children is often transposed by police and news commentators into a mere 'tragic family incident'? Patriarchy did this.

These people hate us! These people are trying to kill us! I don't know why we're all so goddam *nice* about it, but nothing is ever done about the way men carry on. Instead, it's feminism that is for ever in retreat.

~ *Pause to do the dishes.* ~

When any outwardly positive step forward is made, say, toward equal pay or maternity/paternity benefits, something even worse always seems to happen to women on some other level. Patriarchal retribution is swift: for all the mild protests from women against the male bias of Oscar awards, topless photos on

---

telling me you object to joining other women in acquiring all the world's wealth, and thereby subverting the murderous course men have taken during the last five thousand years, because there have existed a few women, real or fictional, with anti-humanitarian sympathies? In other words, because a few creepy women rose to high office *within patriarchy*, you think women as a whole should never be given an even break. But can anyone truly believe women would make as big a mess of power as men have? Come on, who are you trying to kid? Enough of this. We've run out of *time* for ambivalence, hair-splitting, and coquettish self-abnegation. What we need NOW is a radical transfer of power.

3 Why *do* men like pizza so much? I think it's because the boxes look official, as if the guy has just come from some important meeting and he's got really important documents in there or something – whereas really, it's just a big hot slippery blop of dough covered with pepperoni, chicken tikka, and pineapple chunks.

Page 3 of the *Sun*, or nude photos of Jennifer Lawrence shared online, we now have a global rape crisis, with an accompanying boom in female self-harm. Sure, women are permitted to work (great, thanks a lot), and a few hard-working campaigners have managed to deny Britons some *Sun* fun (the exhausting Page 3 campaign eventually paid off, I believe). Women can now sue hackers over invasions of privacy, or even get a prettified portrait of a female novelist on to the ten-pound note (a lot of good this does Jane Austen, who really could have *used* ten quid). But then our punishment comes, in the form of some new, unexpected backlash, along with a multitude of malignant jibes and threats from Twitter trolls. As the much-hounded Mary Beard said in a lecture about men's determined efforts to ignore everything women have ever said over the last few thousand years, women 'pay a very high price for being heard'.[4]

The sources of female oppression are many. Self-inflicted saturation in porn has produced a whole generation of young men who apparently cherish, or at least accept, absurd ideas of pneumatic female torsos,[5] and male rights of domination.[6]

---

4 In the *London Review of Books* (March 20, 2014), Beard described what it's like never to feel you and your kind are properly represented in the culture. NB. America broke away from England for just such a reason: 'No taxation without representation.' Just saying.

5 Our inane absorption in youth and beauty has disenfranchised most of the female population. Never have the ideals of female appearance been so standardised: the self-airbrushed face, the nail polish, the long straight flowing hair, tight-ass jeans, and sassy short top are now compulsory, while the wrinkled, dimpled, frazzled, ex-Pilateased bodies of older women have become the world's last great expanse of uncharted territory.

6 One all too literal 'backlash' against female emancipation is the new allegiance to anal sex, amusingly aired in the aptly named movie *Damsels in Distress* (directed by Whit Stillman, 2012). Men's unwillingness to concern themselves with the clitoris and vagina is a new blight on our age. Corrective instructions on rimming, offered to 'analphobes', suggest any lack of interest in anal sex is inexcusable (adopting a

clockwise direction is highly recommended). And women's increasing dissatisfaction with their own genitals has kept pace with male oversights – when they're done waxing, plucking, and scenting themselves, the next step is creating the 'designer vagina'. Labiaplasty is a growing business, along with a belief that 'abnormal labia tissue' is a widespread problem. The fault is not with pudenda but with misogynists. By the sound of things, men seem to have become worse lovers than ever before (and, given the history of the missionary position, that's saying something!), piteously unaware of their true and ancient role, that of *pleasing women*. Women are not here for male pleasure – men exist to give *women* pleasure. Biology supports this, as Catherine Blackledge points out in *Raising the Skirt/The Story of V* (Orion, 2003/2020), a book highly recommended for anyone interested in female sexuality, or even those who are not – in fact it should be compulsory reading for anyone who purchases a 'sex arse', a rubber sex toy comprising a select portion of amputated torso. ('I voted Leave – but now my sex arses are stuck at customs!', cried a disappointed UK patriot experiencing Brexit shambles – *Sunday Sport Online*, January 2, 2021.) Penis construction throughout nature is oriented more toward *female* pleasure than male, since the quality of the *female* orgasm determines the male's reproductive influence. Even female fruit flies insist on orgasms! (They also have the most elaborate, spiralling vaginas. Who knew?) The vagina, Blackledge reports, is not a passive canal for receiving sperm and issuing offspring. It is an assessment station, selecting and expelling sperm – and one major deciding factor for sperm admission is the female orgasm. People wrongly believe the penis performs 'as a sperm placement tool, a rigid insertion device shaped to shoot sperm quickly and efficiently into the correct orifice'. This fails to explain the varied size and shape of penises, as well as the time and care males of many species take to prepare the female for sperm insertion, throughout courtship and mating behaviour (there's some kind of marsupial mouse that spends *five hours* thrusting – marsupials really know how to live). Despite the standard use of rape in war to secure a genetic advantage over enemies, female pleasure is, if not essential, highly recommended in the passing-on of men's genes. Rape doesn't pay, in the long run, says Blackledge. 'The important question for a male is not: Can I place my sperm inside this female? Rather the crucial question is: Can I persuade the female to use my sperm instead of some other male's?... The primary role of the penis is none other than to act as an internal courting device – shaped to provide the vagina with the best possible and reproductively successful stimulation.' The male orgasm is biologically necessary too, sure, but that's less of an influence on penis construction. All of which reminds me of a limerick:

> There was a young fellow named Prost
> Who tried to make love to a ghost.
> At the height of its spasm,
> The poor ectoplasm
> Cried 'Ah, now I feel it – almost!'

The consequences of recessions[7] are felt most by those already disadvantaged, particularly *women* – in the UK, through cuts to the NHS, rape crisis centres, women's refuges, Legal Aid and other vital services.

Police behaviour toward female victims of crime degrades us all,[8] as does the revealing take on women shown by most news organisations.[9] Despite the notorious 2012 gang rape and

---

7 Disasters caused by men, but borne by women. Men run the banks and building societies after all, the property market, the stock market, industries, Parliament, Congress, the internet, monopolies and corporations and all the other enterprises that keep economic downturns happening. Not only do men create these financial collapses, but they unfairly tend to withstand them better too. *Because they have all the dough!* We are all being crushed beneath their insane belief in growth and progress and maniacal lust for despoiling things. Since the Romans, patriarchy has proved to be the guarantee of a society doomed to implode. (But at least the Romans, before Christianity spoiled everything, had a lot of wine and sex. And chariots. It wasn't all bad.)

8 The accusation of *institutional sexism* must be added to the British police force's proven institutional racism. Only eight out of forty-three police forces in England and Wales respond adequately to instances of domestic violence, according to the 2014 estimate of their *own body*, Her Majesty's Inspectorate of Constabulary. Police behaviour towards purported victims ranges from unforthcoming to shameful. West Midlands police officers called one female victim a 'fucking slag'. 'He threatened to cut my womb out with a pizza cutter. When I spoke to the police, they just laughed,' recalled another abuse victim (*Progress Report on the Police Response to Domestic Abuse*, HMICFRS, November 2017). Predictably, domestic abuse committed by cops is widely covered up by their colleagues, and the victims and witnesses are arrested instead and intimidated. With domestic abuse now on the rise, due to Covid lockdowns, Greater Manchester Police have admitted that they ignored or *erased* seventy per cent of reports of domestic abuse reported during 2020. Not very nice of them. (NB. The police did nothing for years about reports of Jimmy Savile's crimes either. Wherever women are ill-treated, children will be too.)

9 When Phil Spector died in prison in January 2021, the death was largely reported as that of a big important gifted and famous music producer whose life happened to end in 'tragedy'. The tragedy was of his own making. He abused women all his life; he waved guns at people, particularly women who rejected him. He bullied his ex-wife, on pain of death, into accepting an old car and minimal alimony as part of the divorce settlement. And, finally, he shot an actress in the head, whom he'd just met, and then claimed she'd committed suicide in his house. Yet *Rolling Stone*

evisceration in India, quickly followed by a similar event in South Africa and the Steubenville case in Ohio – in which an unconscious sixteen-year-old girl was carried naked from party to party to be sexually preyed upon and peed upon (which some of the participants claimed to have believed was consensual sex) – doubt only seems to grow about what constitutes rape or whether it even exists.[10] The worse men behave, the more their crimes seem to get downgraded to minor misdemeanours. This perversity is necessary to maintain the perverse status quo, the mass delusion which holds that men are okay and women, in so many ways, aren't. How about the sex-slave trade, or the treatment of women and children in detention centres?[11] Such cruelties are not confined to the USA. The English family court system vilifies mothers, shrouds its own proceedings in secrecy, and often issues irrefutable orders, handing children over to

---

treated this recurrent behaviour as incidental, tweeting about 'Phil Spector, the famed "Wall of Sound" producer… whose legacy was marred by a murder conviction' (January 17, 2021). Some legacy.

10 Nitpicking about rape definitions is so wearying, especially when you need all your strength for fleeing rapists. Whoopi Goldberg added to the confusion in 2009 by declaring that Roman Polanski isn't guilty of 'rape-rape'. What, just 'rape' then? Trump seems even more oblivious to all the rape allegations against him, an invincibility that must give new vigour to millions of fellow rapists. In England and Wales, few sexual molestation victims expect any solution from the criminal justice system: rape prosecutions are at an all-time low. Recent figures suggest that only 1.5% of rape claims result in any charge at all (see Julie Bindel, *The Guardian*, January 24, 2021). That's a lot of consequence-free violation going on.

11 Intolerance toward immigrants and foreigners closely resembles the negative male treatment of women and animals and other groups that are left out of calculations except as objects of blame. According to Teresa Hayter, *all* border controls are counterproductive and unjust: 'Their object… is to exclude poor people, and especially black people. The denial of free movement across frontiers gives rise to some of the worst and most vicious abuses of human rights, and provides perhaps the most fertile terrain for the agitation of the far right.' From *Open Borders: The Case Against Immigration Controls* (Pluto, 2004).

unpredictable fathers.[12] The aim of all this is to traumatise women and subdue them. This is traditionally accomplished both through rape, but also through the labyrinthine workings of the justice system.

~ A pause to hang up washing. ~

This is a society that's failing women big time![13] A society in which men keep women in a simmering state of *terror*.[14]

---

12 The UN's Special Rapporteur Rashida Manjoo's statement on sexism in the UK (April 15, 2014) dropped like cool rain on a desert, and even managed to affront the *Mail* (or was it the *male*?). Amongst many acute observations about Britain's non-compliance with the Convention on the Elimination of All Forms of Discrimination against Women (to which, incidentally, the British government had already signed up), Manjoo raised concerns about the machinations of the family court system. She said it ignores 'children and women's safety when hearing applications for contact with estranged parents. ... Lawyers and magistrates have limited understanding of the dynamics of domestic abuse and force children and their mothers to enter into unsafe and inappropriate contact arrangements, which are mostly unsupervised. Shared parenting is increasingly seen as an appropriate, default position without the adequate consideration of the best interests of the child principle and ignoring the history of family abuse...' The best interests of children rarely seem much of a priority in Britain.

13 We think we treat women *okay*? Then why do they feel they have to wear six-inch heels to work? And that their only purpose in life is to sculpt their eyebrows, give good head, and learn to lap-dance? Why does Melania Trump have to organise those 'fucking' Christmas decorations? Why do some women feel they need plastic surgery in order to look like a Barbie doll? This form of self-mutilation is becoming the *norm*, and is now being sought at an earlier and earlier age (if you can afford it, that is; and, if you can't, you may well be fired, demoted, dumped, snubbed, harassed, or shunned). Discrimination on the basis of how you look has long been an effective repressive weapon against women. Every cosmetic procedure performed puts pressure on *other* women to submit to body enhancements. When the fact is, even if you miraculously manage to be whatever's considered beautiful in your era (the ideal is always changing), you'll *still* be stuck in a sexist society that hates you! Women's self-esteem is in *tatters*, smothered under a deluge of photoshopped celebs, the grotesqueries of the designer fashion parade, the realities of poverty, and a gushing river of porn and big-eyed, big-breasted superwoman types in films and cartoon animation, all geared

to prioritise male pleasure and artificial styles of female body. As a result of all this, there are girls on anorexic websites who *congratulate* each other for dying. Why is female life held so cheap? The young opera star Tara Erraught was described in the *Independent* as 'dumpy', by *The Times* as 'unbelievable, unsightly and unappealing', and by the *Financial Times* as a 'chubby bundle of puppy fat'. Ever considered focusing on the woman's *singing* ability? (See Susannah Clapp's great retort to these insults – *Observer*, May 25, 2014.) Why does female fat worry people so? Because it implies a freedom from constraint, a vice, a failure, a lack of decorum. But what heaven does slimness win you? As the novelist Elfriede Jelinek wrote, 'The slim ones, who have worked hard for their figure... climb up the mountains every day or climb the walls at home...' (*Greed*, 2006.) One defect of Susie Orbach's book *Fat is a Feminist Issue*, by the way, is that it offers diet advice: this seriously undermines the radicalism of its empowerment message. It's *fattism* that is the real feminist issue. Meanwhile, in 'The Obesity Era' (*Aeon* magazine, June 19, 2013), David Berreby suggests that being overweight may actually be caused by global *pollution* rather than shameful lapses in self-control. This places guilt back where it belongs, in patriarchy's lap, as the instrument of all this environmental destruction.

14 No one has so far questioned my use of the term 'terrorism' to describe all the really lousy stuff men do to women en masse as a gender – perhaps because the word is so self-evidently spot on. But it all depends on who's doing the defining. Men, the current controllers of language, seem reluctant to admit that all men in a patriarchal society are terrorists. Instead, they trip all over themselves trying to keep the definition of terrorism fuzzy. White American males rarely commit it, apparently. The police and media hesitate to name their barbaric acts 'terrorism'. Nobody even bothered to keep an eye on Anthony Quinn Warner, though his girlfriend warned police a year before his 2020 suicide bombing in Nashville that he was making bombs and plotting some destructive act. Instead, CNN reported after the incident, 'The man who detonated an RV bomb in downtown Nashville early Christmas morning was a loner with no significant criminal record and as yet no signs of a political ideology' (Eric Levenson, CNN, December 30, 2020). Here's what his ideology was: patriarchy. The US Department of Defense's dictionary of military terms defines terrorism thus: 'The calculated use of unlawful violence to inculcate fear; intended to coerce or to intimidate governments or societies in pursuit of goals that are generally political, religious, or ideological.' According to FBI special agent Doug Korneski, terrorism is 'the use of force or violence in the furtherance of a political or social ideology' (Levi Ismail, News Channel 5, Nashville, December 28, 2020). What is *male oppression* if not a coercive campaign that depends on propaganda, blackmail, and the calculated use of unlawful violence to further its ideology? Through violence, or the threat of it, patriarchal terrorists indoctrinate, malign, silence, subdue, guilt-trip, and murder. Misogyny can be *lethal*. Just because this particular terror agenda has been in play for thousands of years doesn't absolve it of criminality. ALL VIOLENCE IS A TERRORIST ACT. Unless committed in self-defence or to protect life. All violence

Yet how we bustle around, trying to *look* good, *be* good, restrain ourselves in all kinds of ways, contort ourselves and our own needs and beliefs in order to work within this set-up men have moulded to suit themselves, in which women are for ever doomed to be the losers, hangers-on, the butt of jokes – funny nutso floozies that we are.[15] The first suggestions the internet offers when you google the word 'women' are: women's clothing, women's shoes, women's dresses, women's trainers. Have we no other interests,[16] no other qualities, no depths? We certainly aren't supposed to.

---

aids patriarchy. And all violence is a hate crime against women, since *women* gave birth to the people being murdered or mutilated, and *women* are usually the ones left to tend the wounded and mourn the dead. Family annihilation, that euphemistic term for massacring the people closest to you whenever you feel like it, is a good example. Killing your family out of pique is not just an unfortunate offshoot of domestic disharmony, as in 'it takes two to tango' and other victim-blaming guff. It is an intimidating display of male power, a misogynistically motivated hate crime, an act of patriarchal terror. The truth will out. The *New York Times* has now introduced the clumsy term 'male supremacy terrorism' (March 17, 2021) and even Wikipedia has a page on 'misogynistic terrorism'.

15 In *The Kreutzer Sonata* (1889), Tolstoy's narrator Pozdnyshev complains bitterly that the whole world is *pro-woman* – essentially because women are big shoppers. There are all these products, he says, aimed at women: they may be hopeless at making money, but they sure can spend it. This picture of male victimhood is neatly contradicted later on though, when it emerges that Pozdnyshev has murdered his own wife in a jealous rage. Mrs Pozdnyshev has had her last spree.

16 Women have to be kept on their toes, worrying and consuming, to keep late capitalism afloat. So-called fashion is a way of corralling women's psyches into acquiescence, even to the point of personal financial ruin. There is continual pressure on women to throw out one set of clothes in favour of another, at great cost to the environment, or risk humiliation. Marks and Spencer released a self-satisfied ad campaign in 2014 called 'Leading Ladies', which involved well-known, middle-aged women like Emma Thompson, Annie Lennox and others, swanning about distractedly in M & S gear (*S & M* gear would have been more appropriate, given the slavish predicament of the fashion-conscious). Somehow, these celebs all seemed a lot more celebratable *before* they were roped into modelling those dopey black-and-white duds. Again, a vague 'advance' made by women (in this case, excelling as actors, artists, movers and shakers) is somehow twisted into its opposite,

~ *Pause to mess — in vain — with my hair.* ~

The media's harsh treatment of Mary Beard, Greta Thunberg, and others shows the high level of hostility directed at women whose achievements single them out from the crowd.[17] This,

---

in the service of commerce. So, instead of offering middle-aged women reason to feel somewhat proud of themselves for what they've accomplished through talent and hard work, M & S's 'Leading Ladies' adverts implied that whatever lofty things these high-flyers may once have had on their minds, what they *really* care about is towing the line in very conventional clothing. For marketers, respected public figures become just more gals on which to hang products. The hidden purpose of it all is to reduce any supposed independence in women to signs of compliance – in this case, compliance with the dictates of fashion. These 'Leading Ladies' weren't leading the way anywhere but the fitting room.

17 Gallantry is dead. In 2013, the BBC sports reporter John Inverdale felt his negative estimation of tennis star Marion Bartoli's feminine allure was required by the nation the day she won Wimbledon. Not very sporting of him. Here is Inverdale on the champion, in her moment of glory: 'I just wonder if her dad did say to her when she was twelve, thirteen, fourteen maybe, "Listen, you are never going to be, you know, a looker. You are never going to be somebody like a Sharapova, you're never going to be five foot eleven, you're never going to be somebody with long legs, so you have to compensate for that. You are going to have to be the most dogged, determined fighter that anyone has ever seen on the tennis court if you are going to make it," and she kind of is.' The message was clear: get back to your mirrors, girls. Because, however good you may be at something else, your only real function in life is to be found attractive by jerks like Inverdale. The BBC received seven hundred complaints about Inverdale's comments (and even a reprimand from Maria Miller, the Tory Secretary of State for Culture, Media and Sport – though what induced compassion in a Tory, I do not know). Inverdale apologised later for his obnoxiousness, and the BBC issued this grudging statement: 'We accept that this remark was insensitive and for that we apologise.' But what good was that? The damage was already done to the psyches of women and girls across the country! The last resort of the cornered misogynist is often hypochondria. Behind every male fist, every declaration of male displeasure, there is always the threat of self-pity. Inverdale claimed illness had interfered with his judgement. Harvey Weinstein succumbed to back trouble (after all his lively antics in hotel rooms too!), travelling to his 2020 trial in a wheelchair. And in June 2014, Michael Fabricant used novocaine confusion (he'd just been to the dentist) as his excuse for his threatening tweet about Yasmin Alibhai-Brown: 'I could never appear on a discussion prog with [her.] I would either end up with a brain haemorrhage or by punching her in the throat.'

after the centuries it took us to get the vote![18] This, after people have *died* to protect abortion rights. After governments across the globe have finally recognised the injustice of female circumcision.[19] What did all these struggles mean?

Not a goddam thing. The violence continues, as does the inequality, and the pay gap,[20] and the production of about a million Hollywood movies that don't pass the Bechdel test.[21] When we peer up through that glass ceiling what we see are the soles of a lot of big dirty men's shoes still galumphing around.[22]

---

18 While American women got there a little earlier, British women were only fully entitled to vote, at age 21, in 1928 – just ten years before the publication of Woolf's *Three Guineas*. (Women couldn't vote in Switzerland and Bangladesh until 1971, and in Iraq had to wait until 1980.)

19 Although the only FGM conviction to succeed in Britain so far occurred in 2019; three other cases ended in acquittal. Meanwhile, a form of *virtual* FGM goes on at Evangelical 'Purity balls' (now spreading to Europe from America). At these cheery gatherings, the sacrificial victim, a teenage girl, dressed all in white, pledges her virginity to her father (eeeugh!), in his capacity as 'High Priest in the home'. I am not kidding. Proffering her virginity to her dad for safekeeping, the girl effectively neuters herself (temporarily) for the sake, she's led to believe, of *another* bloke: her future husband. Not even kissing is allowed in this community before marriage. Weirdly borrowing abortion lingo, the doting fathers, or 'High Priests', claim to be protecting their daughters' 'choice'. What a tangle of hypocrisy, when in fact *any* worship of virginity is a denial of female sexuality and bad news for women.

20 The Equal Pay Act was passed in Britain in 1970, yet it is still unlikely that any woman now working in the UK will see pay equality in her lifetime. The pay gap for British women is currently twenty per cent below men.

21 The modest requirements of the Bechdel test: (1) A movie has to have at least two women in it, (2) who talk to each other, about (3) something besides a man (bechdeltest.com).

22 Despite seven women successfully suing the *New York Times* in 1974 for sex discrimination in hiring, pay, and promotion, the paper has never outgrown its male bias. In 2014 the paper fired its first female executive editor, Jill Abramson. Curiously enough, *Le Monde* fired *its* first female editor Natalie Nougayrède the same week. What unanimity! Female CEOs are more likely to be fired, and fired sooner, than their male counterparts (Edward Helmore, *Observer*, May 17, 2014): male bosses are given more time to settle in, while employers, colleagues, and junior staff are swift to grow impatient with female bosses. Female politicians are

Even Mary-Kay Wilmers defended her *London Review of Books'* lack of articles by and about women, on the grounds that men make more pitches and women have a lot of housework to be getting on with.[23]

~ Pause to scrub the stovetop. ~

---

treated with greater scorn too. The murderous venom directed at Hillary Clinton, Theresa May, Nicola Sturgeon, Angela Merkel, Diane Abbott, Caroline Lucas, Jill Stein, Elizabeth Warren, Kamala Harris, Kshama Sawant and Alexandria Ocasio-Cortez are examples of this intolerant attitude towards women who wield some power in the public sphere. But the harshest treatment of all has been reserved for Greta Thunberg, a *child* who dared to tell it like it is. The fact that she speaks out infuriates a lot of men. One attack came in the form of a cartoon depicting her being raped. Thunberg's unflinching response was: 'This shows we're winning.' (If only.)
23 In an interview conducted by *PN Review* (2001), Wilmers said: 'I think women find it difficult to do their jobs, look after their children, cook dinner and write pieces. They just can't get it all done. And men can. Because they have fewer, quite different responsibilities. And they're not so newly arrived in the country. They're not so frightened of asserting themselves. And they're not so anxious to please. They're going to write their pieces and to hell with the rest. And I don't think women think that way.' ('Why the LRB Should Stop Cooking Up Excuses Over Lack of Women Reviewers', *Guardian*, February 25, 2014.) As of 2015, eighty-two per cent of the articles in the *LRB* since its inception were by men (although it did also publish Mary Beard's lecture on the silencing of women, mentioned earlier). In *Three Guineas*, Woolf warns against such gender segregation, citing the enthusiasm that Hitler and Mussolini shared for the practice. Dictators thrive on division. So, ideally, men should perhaps review women's books and vice versa – if that is the only way to prevent women from being ghettoised. The *LRB*'s track record seems fairly progressive though, compared to the androcentric nonsense churned out by most Saturday newspaper supplements, in which all women seem able to do is eat noodles and model clothing. Most of the columnists, the gardening experts, chefs, travel advisors, car reviewers and other know-it-alls, are men! The self-aggrandisement of male chefs is particularly irksome – women cooked breakfast, lunch and dinner for thousands of years without any fandango. The worst thing about men taking over the cooking of fancy food in restaurants is that every dish now arrives covered in ejaculate, all drizzle, foam, and schmeers. Wait till male gardeners figure out how to make *plants* produce froth – just think of all the prizes, TV spots, and Chelsea Flower Show medals they'll hand themselves.

So, let's admit it. We've tried equality and it *doesn't work*. Equality within a society concocted *by and for* men? Phooey! What we need, what the victims of war and war crimes[24] need, what the terrorised need, what the isolated, and frequently annihilated, radioactive nuclear family needs, what all the tormented, neglected, broken, hunted, infected, injected, vivisected, near-extinct, factory-farmed, in fact *all animals*, need, what every living thing threatened by disease, disrespect, disheartenment, 'detainment', and disenfranchisement, needs, is *female supremacy*.

We can do this the easy way or the hard way.[25]

Veneration is the only *logical* response to the mammalian female. Motherhood is a necessity of survival, and I suspect its offshoot, matriarchy, was a blast. People had it good there for a couple of hundred thousand years, living in stable societies with a three-hour working day and plenty of leisure time. Free to think and act without fear, women invented agriculture, pottery, weaving, music, metallurgy, medicine, painting, sculpture, and astronomy.[26] Then men loused everything up,

---

24 Why *distinguish* between war and war crimes? They are the same thing. WWI veteran Harry Patch said war is 'nothing better than legalised mass murder' (*The Last Fighting Tommy*, 2008). For Thomas Bernhard, war was just further proof of male iniquity: 'War is the poetry of men, by which they seek to gain attention and relief throughout their lives... They [flee] from one misery to another, one misfortune to another, each one deeper and more inescapable than the last, and they always [make] sure of taking someone else with them' (*Gathering Evidence*, 1985).

25 See Valerie Solanas's *S.C.U.M. Manifesto* (1967) for a semi-jokey description of the hard way: S.C.U.M. stands for the Society for Cutting Up Men. But I myself advocate only peaceful methods of revolution. Violence is so *male*. The hell with it.

26 Elizabeth Gould Davis' *The First Sex* (Penguin, 1972) pieces prehistory together through a study of myth, anthropology, and archaeology, to find a predominantly matriarchal past that lasted tens of thousands of years. This, and Marija Gimbutas' archaeological work on widespread and highly creative prehistoric matriarchal cultures in Europe, give one hope that patriarchy was never inevitable, having lasted a fraction of the time that matriarchies persisted; and that there are better, fairer, and much more artistic ways to organise ourselves, i.e. with the focus on WOMEN.

53

driven by fear and envy (of women) and an unquenchable longing for organised sports.

~ Pause to darn a cheap sock. ~

Vengefully appropriating or negating all the progress women had made, men turned on nature and ecology, and instituted a bunch of lousy ideas: anti-female religions and taboos, hatred of the body, particularly female bodies, a paternalistic approach to medicine, and new pastimes like imperialism, slavery, witch hunts, war, rape, drug cartels, vampires, football, darts, and Monopoly. The Industrial Revolution was no picnic either – in the last few centuries, men have managed to ruin the environment for everyone, leaving us with toxic waste, climate havoc, smog, sweatshops, suicidal workers, traumatised pigs, chickens, elephants, and whales, crazed gunmen, conspiracy theories, and a zillion T-shirts that say things. Men have disastrously assumed the right to mess with the air, the water, the land, and our heads.

They are so *messy*, always wrecking things. They like to desecrate things for desecration's sake. They obliterate beavers so they can build their own dams! They shot dead the first grey wolf seen in Iowa for almost a hundred years, despite its being a 'protected' species (protected how?). They shoot lions and tigers, kick chickens.[27] Men denude the land. Men insist, INSIST, on killing everything and using up every last natural resource. War is the quickest way they've found to ruin the environment,[28] but they make peacetime pretty damaging too:

---

27 'Workers at a KFC and McDonald's supplier punch, kick and stamp on the heads of live poultry,' reported the *Daily Mirror* (August 12, 2016).
28 Warring is a classic male trait (noisily mimicked by the ridiculous male absorption in team sports). As Virginia Woolf writes in *Three Guineas*, directly addressing men:

do we really need cars and planes and air conditioning and six trillion throwaway pens and toothbrushes? Does every last thing have to be made out of plastic or concrete? Must the world be so UGLY? San Francisco Bay is still full of mercury from mining processes used during the Gold Rush, and will remain poisoned for the next ten thousand years.[29] The psychotic male addiction to nuclear power, concentration camps, waterboarding, fracking, lead, WMDs, surveillance, TV, computers, the internet, reversing-vehicle beeps, and bling, will finally destroy us all.

Why should we let those Bushes (Sr. and Jr.) get away with it? Or that warmonger Tony Blair? Why'd we let *Hitler* get away with it? Why should we let Jimmy Savile and Rolf Harris and Mel Gibson and Charlie Sheen and Ike Turner and Richard Nixon and Donald Trump get away with it, or Charles Manson, Fred West, Peter Sutcliffe, Thomas Hamilton, John Worboys, and Adam Lanza? Or Ronald Lee Haskell, who executed four children and their parents in their home in Texas, just to get back at his ex-wife. Or Stephen Paddock, the creep who shot sixty people from a hotel in Las Vegas. Not to mention IS and Boko Haram and the *Charlie Hebdo* slaughterers. Why should we let ANY of them get away with it? We can't. *Basta.*[30] And yes,

---

'Obviously there is for you some glory, some necessity, some satisfaction in fighting which [women] have never felt or enjoyed.' But she admits that Wilfred Owen did not share in this penchant. And then there's Harry Patch. And Thomas Bernhard. And all the men who refused to fight in the Vietnam War. And the Veterans for Peace who did fight but now declare: 'We, having dutifully served our nation, do hereby affirm *our greater responsibility* to serve the cause of world peace.' (My italics.) So, the male taste for war *can* apparently be overcome.

29 In fact, it's getting worse, not better! (Douglas Main, *Live Science*, October 29, 2013.)

30 I do, *sort* of, realise that *most* men are not directly, personally responsible for all the atrocities committed by other men; nor do women have an absolute monopoly on humanity and compassion. Women can be fucking mean! It's the kind of animal humans are. We're carnivorous, conflicted, spiteful (and not reacting well, I suspect,

I know, I know, women sometimes go along with some of this stuff. They shoot guns, they work for oil companies, they join extreme right-wing groups, they chit-chat in the Quiet Coach.[31] But that is no excuse for indulging *men* further! Never mind what women may or may not do – it's time for *men* to be mensches.[32]

In *Three Guineas* Virginia Woolf raises the possibility that patriarchy's based on 'unconscious sex-taboos'. But I think, if we're going to get fancy about it, what we're dealing with is more like mass hallucination. Among many other forms of wilful intoxication (are most adult men ever really sober?), men are drunk on self-delusion. Look at Trump: everything he says is the exact opposite of the truth. Merely by dint of their psychoses, their ridiculous conundrums (what pickles men get themselves into!), and their upper-body strength, men have forced women to engage with all sorts of surreal ideas about how life should be lived, from flirtations with nuclear warhead gaps to who gets to decide if women have babies, or how you make an omelette.[33] They have fashioned a whole theatre of the absurd, an extensive literature of alienation, and a great many cowboy movies.

But when do *women* get to dream? How about allowing *us* a

---

to our acute population density). But whatever the failings of women may be, this is no reason for men to be excused from the chore of making amends. The endgame we currently face was inflicted on us entirely by *patriarchy* and its unwillingness to live in harmony with nature – deforestation contributed to the Ebola outbreak, for example: 'Experts say the rising number of emerging viruses is largely the result of ecological destruction and wildlife trade... It doesn't have to be this way.' ('Hunting for "Disease X"', CNN, December 24, 2020.) Clearly, as a 'class' (Woolf's term), men have bungled things badly and *they should set them right*.

31 Still, ninety-eight per cent of mass shootings have been carried out by men.

32 (Or 'menschen'?) In *The Apartment* (directed by Billy Wilder, 1960), C. C. Baxter is urged by his doctor neighbour to give up his presumed playboy lifestyle (that has supposedly led to Fran Kubelik's suicide attempt) and behave like 'a mensch – a human being'. Baxter eventually takes the advice.

33 A word to the wise: very hot pan. There's nothing gentle about making an omelette.

few whims too once in a while? How about indulging women in the belief that we *look* okay, or that we're okay mothers and daughters, or that we have okay things to say or do? Women need time and space in which to develop our own particular brand of insouciance, our own hobbies, our own (pro-female) philosophies, our own sexuality,[34] our own *play*, goddammit!

~ A pause to contemplate a Handkerchief Tree
in the Botanical Gardens. ~

Once again, it's up to women to sort this out, I'm afraid. We shouldn't *have* to, we've all worked hard enough already for little if any recompense! But we will have to exert ourselves further, it seems.[35] So here's my *new* solution (since men wouldn't play the game and just hand over their money to women like I told them to): my advice is for women to go on strike, on a private, public, local, national, and international level.[36] Women make

---

34 The multiple orgasm is, after all, one of nature's triumphs. Why waste it? In a woman-centred society, there would be no further denial of the female orgasm.

35 Get things off to a merry start by painting easily erected corrections for street names – Solanas Street, Wollstonecraft Mews, Austen Avenue, etc. – a la artist Jackie Parry's feminised map of Glasgow, 'Women in the City' (2012); Sara Sheridan's book, *Where are the Women?* (2019), which tackles the whole of Scotland; and Rebecca Solnit's Revised New York subway map (*New Yorker*, October 11, 2016). Metaphysical acts of insubordination.

36 Barcelona has had Vaga de Totes feminist protest strikes, and there have been repeated strikes by women in Poland over new abortion restrictions: in October 2020, women put on a powerful mid-Covid strike, in protest against PiS party's draconian anti-abortion laws, the Catholic church, climate change, and patriarchy in general. Good posters, such as 'The government is not a pregnancy, it can be removed.' That's the kind of thing we need now, *globally*, from small, spontaneous gatherings, to bigger shindigs like the 2017 Women's March on Washington, V-Day, and the corresponding One Billion Rising demos initiated by V (Eve Ensler, author of *The Vagina Monologues*). The latter events are an annual public acknowledgement that one third of all women and girls alive today will be raped or beaten – one billion.

up the majority of the world's population so, united, we cannot fail to have an effect. And there will be jolly times later as we begin to enjoy the fruits of our efforts (see footnote 34).

There are three forms of strike I'd recommend: a housework strike, a labour strike, and a sex strike. I can't wait for the first two. While the ultimate object of all three of them is female supremacy, each strike would also focus on adjunct causes in women's interest: (1) environmental and animal justice; (2) peace and nuclear disarmament; and (3) you guessed it, female appropriation of wealth, property and power.[37] These issues are all bound together in the struggle to preserve nature, civilisation, and the better aspects of human culture.

~ Pause to help husband locate his manbag. ~

STRIKE ONE: NURTURE NATURE.

DESTRUCTION OF NATURE IS AN ATTACK ON WOMEN.

The housework strike will be held in protest against climate change and the destruction of the environment. Its slogan? 'How

---

The aim: 'We rise to show we are determined to create a new kind of consciousness – one where violence will be resisted until it is unthinkable.' It's a *celebration* of women, in fact, and its slogan is 'Strike, Rise, and Dance'.

37 When I first published this essay in *The Baffler* in 2015, I said the precise details of the three strikes were still negotiable and invited readers to help set up strikes, hone the bargaining points, and criticise or make amendments to the adjunct causes I propose – via the email address odalisquerevolution@gmail.com, which I'd just created for the purpose. Then I promptly forgot all about that email account, *for five years*, and missed an approving email from V, amongst others. Some organiser, huh? (I check it more often now.)

dare you?' – after Greta Thunberg's admirable 2019 outburst at the UN.[38] Human attitudes toward animals and the natural world are closely linked to male attitudes towards women: they spring from the same classist anti-nature, anti-life assumption that the world is there to be shaped, ravaged, and ruined by people (men), and all living things are there for the taking. (They want to ravage Mars next.) Animals, it has long been assumed, can be exploited, experimented on, and forced to yield their every atom in service to human greed. Ever since Christianity attested our superiority over other creatures, and scientists started up with their loose talk of 'tool-users' and 'higher' and 'lower' mammals, and philosophers chimed in with their capricious notions of instinct vs individuality, animals have been looked on as a commercial resource rather than as living beings in their own right, entitled to a place in the world. Prehistoric matriarchal cultures never conceived of working against nature in this illogical way – they left nature intact for *us* to destroy.

So, Strike One is a protest against patriarchy's rejection of nature, and the way our narcissistic homocentricism leads to the direct abuse of animals, and the indirect abuse of people. Current farming methods are not only cruel to animals but dangerous to humans, causing pollution, contamination, and superbugs.[39] Habitat assimilation and destruction are our legacy.

---

38 Thunberg delivered a searing speech at the United Nations' Climate Action Summit in New York: 'People are suffering. People are dying. Entire ecosystems are collapsing. We are in the beginning of a mass extinction. And all you can talk about is the money, and fairy tales of eternal economic growth. How dare you?' On a similar theme, Fran Lebowitz's advice to the young is to start searching for water, as 'apparently, we drank it all' ('Hall of Records', *Pretend It's a City*, directed by Martin Scorsese, 2021).

39 It's now thought that Covid-19 is unlikely to have begun with a pangolin in a Chinese wet market; it was probably transmitted from bats or farm animals. But

For the sake of the survival not just of the natural world but of human civilisation, women need to withhold their home- and family-oriented labour: stop mothering,[40] stop daughtering, stop wifeing. Stop cooking, stop cleaning, stop taking out the trash, stop making the beds and ordering the pizzas, stop shopping, stop lugging home bottles of booze for men to guzzle, stop gardening, stop ironing, stop washing your hair, stop putting on make-up (in fact, boycott the whole beauty cult[41]). Stop

---

the disruption of animal habitats, with resulting contact between species which formerly kept their distance from each other, is probably ultimately to blame. The emergence of bird flu, SARS, swine flu, variant CJD, and now Covid, seems related to the increasing interest in bushmeat, and farming malpractice. See Ravi Letzter in *Live Science* (May 28, 2020), and the *Meat Atlas* (Heinrich Böll Foundation/Friends of the Earth Europe, 2014), for evidence of the destructiveness of industrial livestock farming. Rachel Carson's outcry, *Silent Spring* (1962), remains a vital treatment of the subject. See also Nikolaus Geyrhalter's documentary, *Our Daily Bread* (2006), a quietly tragic examination of intensive farming. *Fishing* is now intensive too, causing unchecked pain, collateral death and damage, depletion of stocks, and waste, as well as incendiary disputes about international quotas. Whales, dolphins, and sharks are caught 'accidentally' in fishing nets, leading to *repeated trauma* and often death, even when attempts are made to free them. Seals, blamed for eating the fish, are summarily culled, or mangled in the rudders of boats. Meanwhile, the Great Barrier Reef has lost half its corals since 1995 (BBC News, October 14, 2020) and is unlikely to survive. Due to climate change, pollution, and acidification, the oceans are on track for *mass extinctions* this century (Carl Zimmer, *New York Times*, January 15, 2015). WHAT THE HELL IS WRONG WITH US? ARE WE ALL TOO BUSY GETTING LAID TO GET MAD?

40 This strike is not meant as an attack on motherhood. *Men* thrive on deriding women's bodies and reproductive power. This is why childcare, maternity services, abortion, family planning, schools, and parental access arrangements after divorce are so critical in any battle for equality. Laura Mulvey's film *Riddles of the Sphinx* (1977) movingly pinpoints the political implications of childcare provision. When women have control of their bodies and society within matriarchy, these practical matters will be resolved with ease. In the meantime, carry on shielding your children from danger, providing them with food, clothing, and shelter and helping them with their homework, even during the housework strike – since life, health, comfort, security, education, and freedom of movement are all principles we want to protect.

41 We are now totally obsessed with looks in the West. But the meagre delights of our enthrallment to beauty come at the cost of so much *misery*: anorexia, bulimia,

vacuuming and sterilising the cat litter tray and alphabetising the books and paying the bills. Stop making all those pots of tea and coffee for everybody and smelling the milk to see if it's gone off. Stop embroidering cushion covers. Stop doing all the things you do to try to make a nice home for your family. Stop taking care of things. Just stop it! (This won't be easy for most women. It goes against the grain, since women *invented* the home, in prehistory. Women invented *cosiness*. They needed to establish some domestic tranquillity, comfort and security, in which to raise children.)[42]

~ *Another pause, this time to buy artichokes at the local corner shop.* ~

OCD, suicide, the mercenary diet industry and plastic surgery, injuries from tumbling over in high heels, melanomas from sunbathing and tanning salons, the horrors of unaesthetic gymwear, and jokey vocab for aspects of bodies deemed physically deficient according to current mores (turkey neck, muffin top, cankles, bingo wings, spare tyres, love handles, hairanoia, etc.). People are so corrupted by the modern beauty fixation, they now have 'body dysmorphia', not just about their own but *other people's bodies*: we are troubled by *all* bodies and can see only the supposed faults. It's distracting, depressing, and a great waste of energy. There is no real *need* to assess people's appearance all the time. It's rude, it's abusive, it's dull, it's objectifying. It is thus part of a *spectrum of abuse* that ranges from anti-female biases at school and work, to their full-blown expression in rape and murder. Supreme beauty is a rarity, after all, an aberration. We don't all have to aspire to it. Our concepts of beauty are also based on class and race privilege (we're all aware of 'the skin of the rich'). Audre Lorde talked about 'the racist distortions of beauty', and the way 'gorgeous', even in the gay community, used to be decided by white male standards, 'that world that defined us as doubly nothing because we were black and because we were women.' (Speech at UCLA, early 1990s, https://youtu.be/OUXjoBVQkpw.) Therefore, in conjunction with Strike One, I would like to instigate a *one-year moratorium* on any mention of people's appearance. We can chat about other topics for a change. The beauteous would survive a slight lessening of attention and acclaim, and the rest of us could *relax*. After a year of such abstinence I bet we'll be cured of the habit, and be much better conversationalists.

42 For further elucidation of 'cosiness', see *Mimi*, ibid., pp. 24, 32–33, 37, 64, 66, 72, 82, 171, 195, 198–199, 223, 226, 230–231, 234, 273, 294. (Courtesy of the *Mimi* Index, kindly compiled by the writer Suzy Romer, odalisquerevolutionblog, 2014.)

You can put it all on hold for *a little while*, surely, in aid of animals and the natural world. And what a lot of *thinking* time you'll gain.

This strike will only be called off when governments agree to end animal cruelty, fracking, factory farming, and the intensive use of herbicides, pesticides, and chemical fertilisers. Also, pollution, cars, and dependence on oil and freight containerisation – one of the dirtiest practices ever invented. The money saved from all these shady enterprises can be reallocated to childcare provisions. Ten per cent of every man's net income will be devoted to animal welfare and the restoration of natural habitats and rainforests. Or he can remotely adopt a manatee or blue-footed booby. Six-pack plastic rings, in which turtles get tangled, will be banned. And every man must agree to clean the toilet weekly without being asked; and to confine the foaming, schmeering, and drizzling from now on to the boudoir.

STRIKE TWO: NO MORE WAR WORK.

BOMBS, WAR, CIVILIAN DEATH, NUCLEAR WASTE, AND OTHER FORMS OF MANMADE RADIATION ARE ALL ATTACKS ON WOMEN.

In contradiction of all the romanticised notions of women's contributions to war efforts that we've been asked to stomach lately – all those TV shows about selfless or bitchy WWI nurses, all the photographs of women slaving away in munitions factories, all those movies about the bored-to-tears girl patriots of Bletchley Park – war is no place for women. It's very unlikely that this form of mass homicide was ever women's favoured plan of action (though I admit Hitler had to be stopped some-how). People were apparently killing each other with arrows thirty thousand years ago, which is not nice, but outright group warfare only developed on a grand scale once metal weaponry was developed by Bronze Age societies, which were patriarchal.

War is not in women's interest: it is more likely to cur-tail women's freedoms, as well as distress, subdue, frighten, deprive, and annihilate women, through rape, the murder of offspring, and the degradation of animals and the environment. So, at the very least, women shouldn't have to *help* wars happen. They shouldn't have to fight wars themselves, or proudly wel-come home the injured and the dead. They shouldn't have to provide the world with new men and women to be killed and traumatised in combat.[43] War devalues birth: that is its primary function. War is the rejection, *demolition* of women.[44]

~ Short pause to check online for poorly paid part-time jobs. ~

This strike, Strike Two, involves withholding women's labour in the workforce.[45] But the intentions behind the labour strike are

---

43 This motive for refusing to bear children is mentioned in the two women's letters to the *Telegraph* in 1937, quoted by Woolf in *Three Guineas*.

44 Even military marching is bad for women. Female soldiers have been injured by the requirements of marching, which are always oriented to the length of the *male* leg. For further glimpses into such marching, including a chicken who's pretty good at it, see marchright.com. (And for the best *male* marching, see the bersaglieri of the Italian Army's infantry corps. They run while blowing trumpets.)

45 Of the three strikes I propose, I think the labour strike should be the easiest to pull off – because, after all, who wants to WORK? Why should women, any more than *bees*, participate in the Protestant work ethic devised by *men*? A Day Without A Woman was a labour strike staged in the US in 2017 in protest against Trump. If the necessity of women's labour must be proven in such an elementary way as this, then, so be it. Even a strike of a *day* – by all women everywhere – will bring things to a complete standstill. (Theme song: 'Union Maid', Woody Guthrie, 1940.)

to organise not just an objection to war but also to the threats to future life on earth posed by nuclear energy, nuclear waste, nuclear bombs, and nuclear fallout – and the suffering that they have already caused, through genocide, environmental contamination, and cancer clusters.[46] Men insist that these forces are manageable and necessary. They are not manageable and not necessary. A fifth of all environmental deterioration is caused by militarism. Some of the guys involved in creating the atom bomb had the grace to apologise for unleashing this cataclysmic weapon on us all, and ruining all hope for the future, merely to assuage their own scientific curiosity. But such apologies are of no value. Who in hell cares about Robert Oppenheimer's *conscience*, one of the tiniest things in the universe? Nuclear bombs should never ever have been produced.

Employers will soon 'come to the table' (such a nice domestic phrase!) and meet our terms – and think of the delicious sensation meanwhile of a day/week/month/year off. Overwork silences dissent and original thought and destroys physical, emotional and community health. That's what capitalists like so much about it. WoHeLo, short for Work–Health–Love, the motto (and greeting) of the youth group formerly known as the Campfire Girls (now just Camp Fire), may be a slightly better exhortation than 'eat–pray–love' but it makes no real sense, since most work is *anathema* to health and love. Anyway, women have already worked hard enough. For centuries! It's time they took things easy. This is why the Odalisque Revolution will entail much relaxation in cosy surroundings, eating bonbons and wearing harem pants. 46 The Hanford nuclear site in Washington State contains some of the most radioactive material in the world (fifty-six million gallons of it). Closed for the last thirty years, the containment and clean-up effort costs two billion dollars a year. So many people who live near the site get thyroid cancer that the now familiar throat scar caused by thyroidectomy surgery is known as the 'Hanford necklace'. See also *Hiroshima* by John Hersey (1946); John Adams' 2005 opera *Doctor Atomic*; Michael Frayn's play *Copenhagen* (1998); and Stanley Kubrick's film *Dr Strangelove* (1964), which offers a superbly ironic takedown of the hypocrisy and folly of warmongering in the age of the atom bomb. In one scene, US forces fight *each other* beneath a billboard asserting their official ethos: PEACE IS OUR PROFESSION. You can't stifle American bullshit.

Women *told* men this,[47] but war is a way of silencing women – through injury, exile, deracination, disease, starvation, disrespect, poverty, violation, bereavement, sexual frustration, grief, and, to top it off, a tsunami of male punditry, speculation, and decision-making. Twentieth-century warfare's innovation was to direct itself *specifically* at women and children.[48] Militarists claim a million compensatory motives, but as long as women remain the targets and victims of war, warfare remains just one more outlet for misogyny.

Even after *a million* Britons protested against the Iraq War, Tony Blair went on lying his head off to Parliament and everyone else, insisting the Iraq war was called for. He got away with it, and has played his desired role in genocide. He's still running around pontificating on any old thing. One of the demands of Strike Two will be that Bush and Blair and their confederates are tried by the Russell International War Crimes Tribunal, and that, from now on, the only legitimate military body worldwide will be a carefully monitored UN peace force.

A gentler aim of Strike Two is to give anyone who feels his or her life has been blighted by war in any way, a year's paid

---

47 See Terre Nash's documentary *If You Love This Planet* (1982), in which the great anti-nuclear activist Helen Caldicott challenges the official (male) acceptance of nuclear energy and weaponry. Consider too the noble life's work of Sisters Ardeth Platte and Carol Gilbert, in collaboration with the Plowshares movement.

48 Bombs and the suppression of women are passionate bedfellows. Sven Lindqvist's *A History of Bombing* (1999) charts men's deep love of the bomb, and their willingness to make civilians (women, children, and the elderly) its primary targets. Drone strikes are a variation on this sport. And now we have Boko Haram's massacre of 2,000 civilians in Baga, Nigeria in January 2015, the use of girls and boys as suicide bombers, the abduction of schoolchildren, and their reliance on rape, forced marriage, and slavery to achieve their ends. See Abdulwahab Abdulah and Uduma Kalu in *Vanguard*, May 5, 2014, and Helon Habila's short personal account, *The Chibok Girls: the Boko Haram Kidnappings and Islamic Militancy in Nigeria* (Penguin, 2017).

vacation in order to reflect and recuperate (people providing essential services, such as farming and medical care, might have to stagger their years off). This rehabilitation drive should include not only all military personnel, their families, and their victims, but anyone who's *paid their taxes* (so, count Trump out, sorry), since they too have incurred harm: it is traumatic to have your hard-earned money squandered on illegal wars.

~ Pause to sort through a pile of receipts for tax purposes. ~

There is the necessity of ending non-military uses of nuclear energy too. When exploiting atomic energy for 'peaceful' purposes of this kind, men seem prepared to take incredible risks with our lives and the lives of all future entities on earth. This alone is proof that men are unfit, as a sex, to rule. The deluge of nuclear mess they created may never be adequately contained.[49] Nuclear power stations fail horrifically, leaving us with Chernobyl in 1986 and Fukushima in 2011, both theoretically

---

49 Are we really depending on *men* to safely dispose of nuclear waste? What, are we CRAZY? These are people who have to be reminded to take the dog out. You have to beg them to change a poopy diaper. These are people who use every pot and pan and mixing machine in the house when they cook anything and leave the dirty dishes lying all around the kitchen after. 'They don't cover anything when they put it in the fridge,' Harriet the waitress remarks in *Sleepless in Seattle* (1993). 'Hot Particles' and 'buckyballs' from the meltdown at Fukushima will drift around the planet to *the end of time*. The Fukushima plant poured so much contaminated water into the sea, tuna on the West coast of America now have higher levels of radioactive contamination than ever before. (See Makiko Inoue and Mike Ives, *New York Times*, September 30, 2020, on the plan for compensation.) For the latest on nuclear waste containment strategies – strategies that probably won't ultimately work – see Michael Madsen's devastating documentary about Finland's radioactive waste repository, *Into Eternity* (2010). NB. *No* level of radiation is safe – yet, as far as I know, no government has abandoned the idea of nuclear power. Who gave men permission to risk life on earth for all eternity? Did we have a global referendum on this, I can't remember.

preventable. Where will the next mega-contamination incident occur? Hanford? Then there's the risk that vandals, terrorists, saboteurs or mischief-makers could sneak into nuclear power stations and make off with plutonium – this sort of scenario is never mentioned by politicians when they're foisting another bunch of reactors on us and boasting about how cheap and safe nuclear energy is. It's only cheap if *life* is.

This strike will end when all men quit their jobs in the military sector (female soldiers can remain, *if they must*, but only to work for the UN's peace force) and the government agrees to an immediate end to all peaceful *and* military uses of nuclear power. As punishment for belonging to the gender that thought this stuff up, men must also contribute means-tested contributions (ten per cent of their annual net income) to Women's Action for New Directions (WAND), the Campaign Against the Arms Trade (CAAT), Global Zero, Greenpeace, Friends of the Earth, Ribbon International, ICAN or CND. And good luck to us all.

STRIKE THREE: MONEY FOR SEX.

POVERTY IS AN ATTACK ON WOMEN.

As Woolf points out in *Three Guineas*, women have laboured in the home unpaid for thousands of years, while watching all the family money go on *men's* education, *men's* leisure pursuits, men's beer, men's cigars, and men's pizzas.[50] This debt

---

50 'The daughters of educated men received an unpaid-for education at the hands of poverty, chastity, derision and freedom from unreal loyalties… an unpaid-for education that fitted them for unpaid-for professions' (*Three Guineas*).

has now come due. The money must be reallocated to *women*, and until that is done, straight women should withhold themselves sexually from men.[51] *Men* go on sex strike all the time! They are always withholding sex and making excuses for their unpredictable genitalia, in order to keep women docile. Women knock themselves out trying to be attractive, and men still can't get it up. Well, two can play at that game. Now it's our turn! We mustn't be vindictive though. The pure-minded aim of our sex strike is simply to gain the assets, privileges, and power to which all women are entitled. Yes, I'm talking about *the money*. Since men wouldn't give it up voluntarily, they must be forced to hand it over in return for sex. They're always accusing us of being sluts anyway, so this equation should be easy to grasp: no money, no sex.[52]

The first known fictional try-out of this sexual blackmail strategy occurs in Aristophanes' *Lysistrata*. There, a female sexual resistance strategy is employed to bring the Peloponnesian war to an end.[53] Lysistrata enlists the help of both allied and enemy women, on the grounds that the war is bad for *all women*. They

---

51 It would be important to enlist the support of sex workers in this endeavour, since men (*currently*) have the means to buy their way out of sexual privation (something the cheerless incel brigade seems to have forgotten). Financial compensation will be offered to female sex workers, to sustain them through the furlough.

52 Lesbians need not participate in the sex strike. They can protest in other ways. Gay sex in both genders will be unaffected by the strike, or might even enjoy a surge in popularity. That is beyond our control. The purpose of the strike is *male* sexual privation, not female. Heterosexual women will have to handle this temporary hiatus as best they can. I don't agree with Andrea Dworkin, though, that feminism precludes heterosexuality. It's time for the fun to *begin*, not end! (Once all three strikes have succeeded.)

53 *Lysistrata*, by Aristophanes (411 BCE), in *Lysistrata and other Plays*, translated by Alan H. Sommerstein (2002). Spike Lee's fun and moving musical *Chi-Raq* (2015), transposing *Lysistrata* to the gun-filled streets of the South side of Chicago, bolsters the idea that sex can still be used as a major bargaining tool today.

hole up in the Acropolis together and it's really quite a successful sit-in. Some of the women do try to tiptoe off, offering feeble excuses like: 'the moths will be eating my sheepskin,' 'I turn out to be pregnant and have to go home to have the baby – I'll be back tomorrow,' and 'the owls [fellow inhabitants of the Acropolis] are keeping me up at night.' (I paraphrase.) But in the end, the plan works like a charm: the priapic menfolk are soon inspired to agree a peace deal, so they can rush the women back to bed.

Even with the sorry proliferation of porn, sex slaves, and sex arses (see footnote 6) – offering alternatives to men unwilling or unable to engage with female desire – a sex strike still seems a viable ploy with a proud history.[54] For even greater effect, we might try the showstopping power of vaginal display.[55] Such a

---

54 Chris Knight writes about sex strikes in his spectacular book on prehistory, *Blood Relations: Menstruation and the Origins of Culture* (Yale, 1991). Women held a sex strike in Nicaragua in the 1530s, as a protest against slavery, and Igbo women in Nigeria have often scared men with their sex strike power. More recently, the tactic was used in Liberia to protest against the vicious civil war (2003), in Naples in protest against dangerous, illicit fireworks on New Year's Eve (2008), in Kenya (2009), and in Ukraine (2010). The Strike of Crossed Legs worked in Pereira, Colombia (2006/2011), in protest against gang warfare: 'We want them to know that violence is not sexy.' Pereira's murder rate, at the time the highest in Colombia, dramatically declined as a result. In 2011, women in Barbacoas, Colombia successfully used a sex strike to ensure long-awaited road repairs were done. And it was utilised in the Philippines (2011), Belgium (2011 – *proposed* at least, by a socialist senator, if not implemented), Togo (2012), Sudan (2014), and Tokyo (2014), when women threatened not to sleep with any man who supported the corrupt governor Yōichi Masuzoe, who'd proclaimed that women should never hold top roles in government because they're nutty when they have a period (he was later ousted for his misuse of public funds, which he could not blame on menstruation). Femen too has sometimes advocated sex strikes. And a sex strike added an extra dimension to a protest against the Russian presence in Ukraine (2014), publicised with the slogan 'Don't Give It To A Russian'.

55 The vulva's mythic significance as the basis and origin of all human life makes vaginal display the perfect antidote to the male death-lust. In ancient history, women

strike would of course have to be carefully *policed*, because of men's dependence on violence as a means of comment and coercion. Not everyone's as sane and reasonable as Aristophanes' male characters (witness the violent and sexual threats launched at women who dare to speak out about anything).

Now, no shirking, sisters. No lame apologies and secret assignations! Remember, there will be *plenty* of sex (make-up sex!), once men have recognised their responsibilities as human beings, lovers, and *mensches*.

~ Pause to push through hordes of mamas and babies in a cafe. ~

We might also hope for a drop in the pregnancy rate as a result of the sex strike. Parenthood has many profound joys, and should have its rights too (maternity/paternity leave, etc.). It is a traditional and theoretically honourable part of adult life. But having a child doubles your carbon footprint. It's also harder and harder to get close to paintings in museums. A moratorium on childbirth might give women a chance to explore the freedom, leisure, self-containment, and privacy of childlessness. The missing tax revenue and pension contributions that a lower birth rate might cause could be replenished by opening the

---

resorted to vaginal display both as a fertility rite and as a form of protest. According to Catherine Blackledge, *Raising the Skirt*, women in Greek mythology used this method to subdue Bellerophon, who was threatening to flood the Xanthian plain. In addition, 'making derogatory remarks about female genitalia is punishable by vaginal display en masse... in [parts of] Africa'. In a rare acknowledgement of female sexuality, Sheela-na-gigs, those exaggerated ancient and mediaeval stone carvings of women pulling their vulvas wide open (surely a remnant of prehistoric mother-goddess cult symbols), were added to buildings to ward off evil and promote fertility. Femen activists not only use upper-body nudity to shame men, but sometimes go bottomless as well.

borders to more immigration. But this birth pause does not in any way discount the whole history and heroism of motherhood.

Some feminists complain that the concept of a female sex strike implies, dispiritingly, that women have no sexual needs of their own, and that sex is just a commodity that women supply for *men*. No. Nobody has any automatic right to sex. Withholding sex is simply one power women can wield, amongst others, in the service of a good cause. The sacrifice incurred by the sex strike will be borne by *both* sides, in aid of female emancipation. Once matriarchy is established, the needs, wishes, and capabilities of women will finally be given the attention they deserve. We'll have a ball.

The sex strike will only be called off once the majority of men permanently transfer the majority of their financial assets (on an ongoing basis) to one or more women of their choice, or contribute the same on an ongoing basis to a women's charity or non-profit banking organisation formed to issue women loans, such as the Grameen Bank in Bangladesh. Governments must also make all violence a crime, and tax men twice as much as women, the revenues raised to be earmarked for the enhancement of women's lives, in the form of safety, education, free menstruation materials,[56] childcare and reparations for slavery. In addition, schoolchildren must study prehistory in order to get an understanding of matriarchal cultures. So as to reinstate men's natural duty to serve female pleasure, biology courses and sex ed classes in school will work to revise our decayed approach

---

56 Scotland voted in November 2020 to become the first country in the world to provide free menstrual products to all who need them. But there is progress elsewhere too: Canada, Australia, India, Colombia, Malaysia, Nicaragua, Jamaica, Kenya, Nigeria, Uganda, Lebanon, Trinidad and Tobago, and a number of US states have stopped taxing period products.

to sex, with particular emphasis on the female orgasm and the abandonment of porn. Men must spend at least one day a week listening instead to what women have to say. And I wish they'd smile more — men's default facial expressions are too gruff. They frighten me.[57]

~ *Pause to caress husband's cheek.*[58] ~

If all else fails, we can always mobilise a pizza strike. That's *got* to work.

Would we settle for less than the demands outlined here, men might ask. But we *have*, we have, for thousands of years. It's terrible that Virginia Woolf had to settle for less.[59]

---

57 At a small Bloomsday celebration at the Irish consulate in Edinburgh on June 16, 2014, I noticed that all the men there were standing around *scowling*, while the women tried to be genial. This wasn't because the men were having a lousy time (the Guinness was really flowing), they're just LAZY. (What would Joyce have made of it?!) Men really need to acknowledge how threatening the male scowl is. They need to start learning how to adjust their faces into more frequent displays of beneficence. Is it fair for women to do all the giggling and smiling and buttering-up, forever trying to make everybody feel comfortable? Why *should* we, after what we've been through? It's MEN who make everybody uncomfortable, so it's they who should make more of an effort to be friendly. Sheesh, do we have to explain every little thing? Just as they can learn not to walk menacingly down a dark street behind a lone woman, they can also master the art of smiling.

58 Husband remarks encouragingly that, once the aims of all three strikes have been realised, capitalism will be kaput.

59 The Mea Culpa Declaration: 'I, the undersigned, confess to having, consciously or not, overtly or not, been part of a worldwide conspiracy that has constrained women's lives through centuries of violence, repression, distress, and discouragement. I recognise that this treatment of women has been a ploy in a power game – the result of male cowardice, stupidity, perversity, cunning, and corruption – and that the status of men has been artificially exalted by it.

I acknowledge that vast numbers of women have been unfairly treated throughout the era of male rule. I therefore apologise for any tyrannical behaviour of my own, and that of other men, and pledge to do my utmost to correct the

_____

problem, and prevent such injuries, insults, and injustices from ever occurring again.

I apologise too for stubborn male resistance over centuries to women's ideas, thoughts, decisions, and remarks –in the home, at work, in business, in the arts, in education, and in government. In light of the loss of valuable female input over centuries, I now agree to abide by the decisions women make, without resorting to mindless criticisms and the usual reflex contradictions and derision, no matter how wacko or whimsical the ideas expressed by women may seem to me to be.

I renounce male power and privilege, on the grounds that they were unsportingly won, and I wish to relinquish all remaining economic, social, and political advantages I may have obtained, either as a mere consequence of being male, or because of my active participation (now regretted) in misogynist behaviour and acts of patriarchal terror, either overt or underground.

In aid of this, I have transferred, or will transfer and *continue* to transfer, my financial resources to a woman or women, *no strings attached*. By such means, I hope to see a societal shift and foster a more humane environment in which women and children are less likely to be mistreated or maligned. It is my hope that the handover of power and property to women will ultimately transform and benefit people, animals, and the natural world, as well as ensuring a future for thought, languages, nature, culture, and the arts.

I believe in the pleasure principle, and therefore renounce the male work ethic as an indecency imposed by men who wished to profit off the subjugation of others. I hereby renounce male privilege and assert the inalienable right of *all* creatures to life, liberty, and the pursuit of happiness.'

SIGN HERE: _____

73

A SPELL
OF PATRIARCHY

In the days before Covid, when thought ranged free and queuing wasn't lethal, I was standing in line at a cheese shop, contemplating our dependence throughout life on *milk*, mothers' milk (and all the other kinds, like cow, goat, sheep, buffalo, almond, oat and soya), when it occurred to me that the Hitchcock movie I'd just watched, *Spellbound*,[1] is really about sexual harassment. It's *not* about Gregory Peck's ridiculous psychological problems; it's really about *women's* problems – with men. It's a #MeToo movie from seventy-five years ago. Whether he meant it this way or not, Hitch was ahead of his time. Maybe his conscience was bothering him?

Notoriously keen on hiring blonde actresses, for personal and pragmatic reasons – blondes at the time were box office gold – Hitchcock was no feminist hero. He used (some would say abused) some of the most famous blondes around: Grace Kelly,

---

[1] 1945.

Carole Lombard, Eva Marie Saint, Tippi Hedren, Joan Fontaine, Doris Day, Janet Leigh, Kim Novak, and Ingrid Bergman. Oddly, he settled on Hedren for both *The Birds* and *Marnie*, an awkward actress at best, brittle and shaky. But still – a blonde. Yet, for all his Pygmalionic tendencies, and for a guy who spent so much time just trying to *scare* people, Hitchcock's portrayals of women can sometimes be surprisingly generous and sympathetic.

He also really knew how to make a movie, at least most of the time – his flop/gem ratio is pretty impressive. I had largely forgotten *Spellbound* when I saw it again, and enjoyed every minute. Though completely absurd, it's now joined my list of Hitchcock must-haves, along with *North by Northwest*, *The Lady Vanishes*, *Rear Window*, *Strangers on a Train*, *Mr & Mrs Smith*, and *The 39 Steps*. I can watch *The Birds*, too, even *Marnie*, once in a while, but they're pretty awful. And *Psycho* is just a joke – what a mess, with that mom and the rocking chair and all. The murder in the shower, a cheap stunt, frightened me every time when I was young, but you already know Janet Leigh is doomed as soon as you see her in her underwear. That amount of vulnerability is code for victim.

For discussion purposes, we could call Bergman and Peck by their fictional names in *Spellbound*, out of respect or something: Dr Petersen and Dr Edwardes. But at this stage of the game, who really thinks of them as anything but Ingrid Bergman and Gregory Peck? So, to Bergman. She plays a psychoanalyst, and she's not half bad at it. The job really seems to suit her. She could've helped even Hitchcock. She's not just well-trained and studious, she's bursting with snappy put-downs that help her thread her way through the forest of obnoxious men she's up against.

Hitchcock was such a sucker for proclamations about psychology, many priceless jewels of corniness are on display in his work. *Psycho* ends with one, just to make things feel even more ridiculous than they already did. *Spellbound* begins with one, and it's a classic of the genre, informing us earnestly that psychoanalysis 'treats the emotional problems of the sane'. The only trouble with this assertion in this movie is that most of the characters in *Spellbound* really are out of their minds. The shrinks are as wacky as the patients.

One principle of psychoanalysis is that what's buried deep in the unconscious will pop out in some way, no matter how well you try to repress it. It's a process of opening locked doors in the subconscious. Actual doors open for Ingrid Bergman in *Spellbound* – not *professionally*, natch, but in her head, when she starts to fall in love with Gregory Peck. To be fair, this was 1945, the bumpy start of psychoanalysis' heyday. Hollywood was full of shrinks (and locked doors, too, come to think of it). But the real craziness buried in *Spellbound* is not the libido, romantic love, mental collapse, nor the mysterious source of Peck's baffling complexes, but *misogyny*. The movie veers off from Peck's mental disorder to become an examination of everyday sexism: what it's like to be a woman tormented by men. For, wherever Bergman goes, she's under male scrutiny, if not direct attack.

On the surface, the story concentrates on Gregory Peck's mixed-up identity and amnesia and phobias and fainting spells and stuff, but you soon sense that Peck's psychological disintegration is by the by. The movie is told from *Bergman's* point of view, and what's really memorable about it are the difficulties *she* faces (Hitchcock was probably one of them). You can tell Peck doesn't matter much, by the way the three sensationalised crises of his life are handled so breezily. They turn out to be 'MacGuffins' (not a new fast-food breakfast item, but Hitchcock's word for the intentional distractions he liked inserting in his movies). What matters here is *Bergman*. Of course. I mean, you get Ingrid Bergman on screen, the movie's going to be about Bergman!

Here is a woman rising fast in a male-dominated profession. Dr Petersen is the Ruth Bader Ginsburg of psychoanalysis, a whizz-kid, and analytically sensitive up the wazoo. Hitchcock awards Bergman's character some genuine heroism as a career woman. She's so beautiful that her colleagues seem reconciled to having a female in their midst. But they don't *like* it, and they're constantly making gendered digs about her. They seem to have all the time in the world to mess her around. One pest likes to criticise her for her apparent asexuality. Because she rejects *him*, he accuses her of frigidity, that old salve to the male ego. He says touching her is like embracing a textbook, laddishly warns, 'Your lack of human and emotional experience is bad for you as a doctor. And fatal for you as a woman.' But Bergman's ready with the cutting riposte: 'I've heard that argument from numerous amorous psychiatrists who all wanted to make a better doctor of me.' Touché.

She seems to be the only professional in the whole institution. She *has* to be – her colleagues are all lazybones and chauvinists who tell her things like 'The mind of a woman in love is operating on the lowest level of the intellect,' and 'You're an excellent analyst, but rather a stupid woman.' Why don't you quit harassing her, you jerks? Just go straitjacket somebody or something. She's the best shrink in the place! It's pretty amazing Bergman ever gets a thing done, with all these malingerers hounding her. But she does, and she appears to be a genuinely good analyst: she takes on Peck of all people – a bundle of nerves, suffering from a bad case of impostor syndrome, amnesia, and PTSD, not to mention a crippling fear of whiteness and black stripes – and she 'cures' him.

Hitchcock's ideas on psychology are amusing throughout. They're highly physical – with him, it's never just about people's *thoughts*, there's always some violent dramatic experience at the heart of things, which has to be exposed. He equates neuroses with constipation and treatment is all about administering a good fig syrup of flashbacks. What's required, emetically, is for the patient to fully remember the trauma and expel it. So, to get well, Gregory Peck has to relive the three incidents that have cumulatively unhinged him – firstly, a childhood blunder, in which his brother got impaled on a fence after Peck accidentally pushed him off a wall; secondly, an injury during WWII, caused when he was an Air Force pilot and his plane was shot down; and finally, the quite recent sight of his psychiatrist skiing off a snowy peak to his death. (I don't know why anyone skis. Bergman herself has to ski later in the movie, very riskily, so as to stir memories in Peck. But she's Swedish, so she's good at it.)

Bergman's task is to figure all this out, and fast (before Peck ends up in prison), and she can do it too, but not without alienating every man she encounters – even Peck, though he's crazy about her. In their first encounter, she tries to draw a picture on a white tablecloth with the tines of her fork and Peck goes all woozy. We don't know why yet, except that the marks she makes are strikingly vulval in shape. Peck's aversion to the drawing adds a telling note of misogyny to his other quirks. Making things even more suggestive, he tries to rub the lines on the cloth out with a knife, the blunt blade urgently nudging the notional labia. The perfect start to a great romance!

Before she sorts Peck's pecker out, I mean his psyche, Bergman falls in love with him in a big way: the movie's full of kissing scenes. This development mixes interestingly with the therapeutic job at hand. One minute, she's wondering why the pinstripes on her bathrobe freak him out, the next they're kissing. One minute they're deftly evading the police at Penn Station, next they're necking again. And along the way, Peck's contempt for women bubbles up whenever Bergman pokes her nose too skilfully into what's bugging him. 'If there's anything I hate, it's a smug woman!' he snarls. She pooh-poohs this sort of remark as the inevitable annoyance an analyst rouses in the wary patient. She's undeterred, intent on being professional. But she's hurt. Falling in love is actually full of *pain*. This doesn't get mentioned enough.

~~~

Everywhere Bergman goes, sexual harassment follows. As Grace Kelly says in *Rear Window*, 'I'd say she's doing a woman's hardest job: juggling wolves.' *Spellbound* is the story of one woman up against a wall of male authority, from the outside world of male doctors and male cops to her troubled love object. Peck suddenly disappears from the psychiatric facility, fleeing the police. He only tells Bergman the name of the hotel in New York he's heading for. She rushes there, hoping to catch a glimpse of him in the lobby. An addled lech immediately hits on her, smoking his cigar right in her face and squeezing her into a corner of the couch. Peeved but perky, Bergman asks him, 'Do you mind not sitting on my lap in public?'

A hotel detective rescues her from this guy, and then deposits his own load of sexist preconceptions on Bergman. He somehow jumps to the conclusion that she's a sweet innocent teacher in search of her runaway husband. He's made the whole scenario up for himself. Bergman plays along with his fantasy simply to get hold of Peck's room number. Later, when the detective realises he's been had, he's affronted – having been charmed at first by her teacherly naïveté, he now feels slighted by her craftiness. Humiliated. Men are so touchy.

As many a #MeToo accuser has charged, merely by speaking to men, or working with them, or treating them, or loving them, women potentially provoke the most terrible retributions. There's even a hint of domestic violence in *Spellbound*. Early on, Peck threatens to 'biff' Bergman for prodding him with too many questions. And later, when they're staying at her old teacher's house, Peck seems sorely tempted to slit her throat. Why else is he so stirred by the sight of an open razor, why so drawn to stand menacingly over the sleeping Bergman, soft and helpless in the bed?

'He was dangerous,' her kindly mentor confirms the next day, having quietened Peck with a dose of bromide in his milk. Ah, yes, *milk*, that distinctly female secretion! White as snow, white, Snow White,[2] white, white... aaagh! Peck's not good with anything white, yet he drinks up his spiked milk like a good boy. What pops uncontrollably out of Hitchcock here is, on the one side, the mammalian female creating and nurturing life (also insightfully analysing people for free), and on the other, the male urge to kill somebody, *anybody*, for no good reason. These opposing forces battle for control of the love affair, and the movie, if not the whole society.

Psychoanalysis has often despaired of women. Detailing the faults of mothers has worn out the velvet of many an analytic couch. Freud expressed his own exasperation with women in

---

2 She too was overworked and underpaid.

the uncharitable question 'What do women want?' Well, maybe what women want is to *steal the show*, take the floor, regain centre stage, their rightful place in the world *and* in Hollywood films (they already have the upper hand in operas). Echoes of matriarchal prehistory lurk in the collective unconscious, and have a lasting appeal.

Who doesn't want Ingrid Bergman to be happy? We've seen her driven to distraction in nice outfits in so many movies. In Paris, all leggy in that gold dressing gown, just before the Germans invade and everything goes blooey – nothing like the dowdy pinstriped old-maid bathrobe Hitch lumbers her with in *Spellbound*, the vertical lines of which send Peck into a tizzy. We long for Bergman to relax and feel safe! Let's face it, we want her drinking champagne with Humphrey Bogart. Gregory Peck's just a little too complicated.

They work things out, of course. Peck is going to be an effective doctor again, with Bergman at his side. And the goons are gone: she's seen them all off. Patriarchy's only an idea after all, like an evil spell. We're not bound to it.

THIRD-RATE ZEROS

Now that the big fat loser of a president, that tremendously sick, terrible, nasty, lowly, truly pathetic, reckless, sad, weak, lazy, incompetent, third-rate, clueless, not smart, dumb as a rock, all talk, wacko, zero-chance lying liar, phoney, nut job, clown, fraud, con man, hypocrite, lightweight, poor loser, goofball, and low-life Donald Trump is gone (pending prosecution and ignominy), we need to start repairing the *neurological damage* Trump has done worldwide. It's amazing how quickly an undereducated, big-shot hooligan can make you forget there are such things as decency, decorum, honour, truth, kindness, politeness, humour, morality, intelligence, knowledge, justice, democracy, laws, a Constitution, even! And art.

Civilisation, in fact.

A good first step would be for everybody to stop belittling people the way Trump does. That includes attacks on Trump himself for *his* supposed bodily flaws. They are minor compared to his real crimes. People have often highlighted Trump's obesity, a cheap shot and indirectly offensive to millions of similarly afflicted Americans, obesity being something of a national sport. Trump's not alone in wolfing down the KFC and chocolate cake; and being fat is also not the worst vice in the world — unless anorexia's your thing. It's certainly not *Trump's* worst offence — not compared to raping, obstructing justice, killing hundreds of thousands during the corona-virus pandemic, inciting insurrection, and hurrying public executions in his final days in office while issuing pardons for fellow traitors.[1]

Trump opponents raised doubts about his *continence* too, suggesting various accidents and a reliance on 'diapers'. Rumours have circulated about his farting during public appearances (his lawyer Giuliani apparently does it too). But this strategy is problematic, since even contemptible, irresponsible, racist, sexist, fascist, tyrannical and gaseous assholes are still human. Trump has the right to an alimentary canal like everybody else. Criticise him — *please* — for sending immigrant children to concentration camps and losing track of their parents. Send him to jail for life for *that*. Deprive him of his golf bag even. But leave the creep's allegedly fallible anal sphincter out of it. That's playground stuff, caca and peepee. The emissions from his foul mouth leave the more lingering stink.

∿

---

1 One of his final wretched acts in office was to push forward with the execution of Lisa Montgomery, a woman of dubious sanity and the first woman in America to be executed by the federal government in seventy years. This was the eleventh of the thirteen executions Trump rushed to complete during his final gory days in office (*New York Times*, January 13, 2021). Montgomery's lawyer said the execution of her client was not only a superspreader event but a 'vicious, unlawful and unnecessary exercise of authoritarian power'. An ex-classmate of Montgomery's *approved* though, claiming that 'it would definitely help with some closure'. Americans are hooked on closure. And see where it gets them.

Along with all his crassness, volatility, and tragic magnetism, Trump has exhausted us with his exaggerations, his rhetoric, his hyperbole, his suspicions, his attention-seeking, his pronouncements, his pronunciation, his grammar, typos, and tastelessness, his neediness, disrespect, lawlessness, madness, and outright lies. He has defeated us, defiled us, *crushed* us with gibberish – all those animosities of his and his sulks. The grievances, the mood swings, the meltdowns, the firings and hirings, the taunts and conspiracy theories. He has been proved wrong a million times – about the Central Park Five, whom he wanted to execute; about Obama's birthplace – but truth never gets in the way of a Trump moan. Without a shred, a *shred*, of evidence, he insisted that the painstaking efforts involved in the 2020 presidential election, conducted with amazing efficiency and heroism during a pandemic (the pandemic *his* policies exacerbated), was 'the most corrupt election (by far!) in the history of the USA'. Whenever Trump describes what's wrong with the world, he's always unconsciously describing himself, with some accuracy: if he'd said *he* was the most corrupt president (by far!) in the history of the USA, he'd be within range of the truth. If he just admitted that *he* is nasty, *he* third-rate, *he* the swamp that needs to be drained, the whole world could get a better night's sleep.

We will have to make an effort to regain our sanity, and a little modesty in our own use of language. Perhaps think twice before yelling 'You are the goddam stupidest person on the planet' and threatening the most gruesome forms of demise every time someone mentions avocados, Bernie Sanders, J-Lo, rain, memory foam, the Olympics, or, say, Canada. Enough already with the personal attacks, enough with the childish threats. We need a five-year ban on verbal abuse. Hold those adjectives! Here's an idea: replace them with *numbers*. That should lessen demand.

0 = Zero.

1 = Fat.

2 = Second-rate.

3 = Third-rate.

Etc., etc.

11 = Tremendous.

12 = Sad.

13 = Nasty.

14 = Lying.

15 = Dumb.

16 = Wacko.

17 = Clueless.

18 = Phoney.

19 = Goddam stupidest.

Trump, for instance, is a 15, 17, 3, 12, 13, stone-cold loser, 18, and the 19, 14, 16 0. See? Not very satisfying.

∽

Though becoming president may beat the many other inappropriate roles he's assigned himself in life, Trump also considers himself an indispensable judge in an ongoing notional beauty pageant taking place in his own head. The guy critiques every female body that comes his way, including his own daughters'.[2]

---

2 Amazingly, in the midst of his anarchistic campaign to block the outcome of the 2020 presidential election, Trump took time out, just after Christmas 2020, to worry about why 'nasty' Kamala Harris was allowed to be on the cover of *Vogue*, when the robotic Melania Trump had never graced the front of a magazine in the whole four years of her husband's presidency. Why, Trump railed, was Melania so neglected? Uh, maybe because Melania is merely an unremarkable *First Lady*, not the first woman of colour to become vice president? Could *that* be it? Besides which, Melania's sycophancy and baffling fashion statements make everybody vomit.

Instructions on female beauty are a generous extracurricular duty Trump has set himself, for the benefit of humanity. Many men do it, of course – openly or not, they're forever formulating opinions on women's looks and slotting us into position on a scale of 1 to 10.[3] Gay men seem equally busy establishing a consensus on male beauty traits. Immature and extremely insecure, men feel safer all lusting after the same object. Nostalgic men wallow in *memories* of perfect bodies, while men who live in the Now just stand around on street corners evaluating the passing throng, or embark on stalking missions. No one questions why beauty or the lack of it matters a damn.

Conventional beauty is a minor, accidental, and temporary achievement. Okay, it gets you modelling jobs and parts in movies, and occasionally stirs up a pang of envy, ruining a few friendship prospects. Sadly, our tendency to glorify physical perfection decides the fate of many supposedly less beauteous women. But people are more than just physical entities (*some* are, anyway). A lot of them have interesting insights or news items to offer. They also have plans, desires, meaning, lives, and rights. Reducing connections between people to the level of a beauty-based pillow fight diminishes both the judges and the judged. How much time in life and in literature has already been wasted on mean, irrelevant, and soon outdated notions of beauty? You know, *so what* if Cinderella was beautiful and her step-sisters weren't? Is this really *really* the key to an understanding of human capacity? Is it fair? Is it even interesting?

---

3 'Seen any good dicks lately?' the exasperated Texas Governor Ann Richards once asked, after listening to yet another man extol at length the exact virtues of some female acquaintance's body. (The columnist Molly Ivins liked to recount this remark.)

My mother thought it was rude to comment on people's appearance. I agree. Most of the attention we give people's looks is wholly unnecessary unless you're a police officer in search of a suspect. Physical descriptions of protagonists in novels likewise give me the creeps, or send me to sleep. Who the hell cares? *Dickens* can get away with it because he makes the whole business seem like harmless fun. And his plots feature so many characters, he *has* to hand the reader some way of remembering them all. Here he is on Uncle Pumble-chook:

> A large hard-breathing middle-aged slow man, with a mouth like a fish, dull staring eyes, and sandy hair standing upright on his head, so that he looked as if he had just been all but choked, and had that moment come to.[4]

What could be better than that? Succinct and funny, the information is painlessly absorbed. Nobody would want to *be* Pumble-chook, but we excuse it in him. Similarly, Marilynne Robinson playfully conveys one woman's chaotic personality through the way she looks, ending with a top-notch one-liner:

> She had lavender lips and orange hair, and arched eyebrows each drawn in a single brown line, a contest between prac-tice and palsy which sometimes ended at her ear. She was an old woman, but she managed to look like a young woman with a ravaging disease.[5]

---

4 *Great Expectations* (1861).
5 *Housekeeping* (Farrar, Straus & Giroux, 1980).

But more straight-faced physical depictions can be ponderous, clumsy, insulting and inert. I struggle to scramble my way past all the big eyes and lips and cheekbones and nose angles and beauty spots and earlobes and hair colour and dress design and the svelte lines of a million pretty fictional heroines' figures that authors tirelessly line up for our amusement. We're rarely told about these people's fallen arches or faulty immune systems, their borborygmus or their questionable nose-blowing techniques – though these issues could be more pertinent to the way the person approaches life, and more entertaining, than the type of eyelashes they happen to be fluttering. Jane Austen never wasted much space on people's looks: all you need to know is one sister or other was generally considered the prettier. If that.[6]

Women bear the brunt of all this impertinent attention. Hermione Lee brings up the (large) size of Edith Wharton's breasts in her comprehensive biography of the writer – one scholarly intrusion too many?[7] It's usually *male novelists* who need to be forcibly restrained from breast-tracking. Some can't introduce a new female character without jumping to pinpoint, approvingly or not, exactly what her breasts are like – as if this were the pre-eminent issue in any woman's existence. The breasts of *unsexy* female characters are rarely mentioned, as if these lesser figures have been subjected to a wholesale double-mastectomy programme before the typing began. Such writers, intent on

---

6 In *Persuasion* (1818), she satirises Sir Walter's absorption in both his own beauty and the physical flaws of everyone else. 'We are not all born to be handsome,' Mrs Clay cautions helpfully. (Though, soon enough, Austen falls into a trap of her own making, dissing poor plump Mrs Musgrove for the incongruity of being fat and having deep emotions.)

7 Chatto & Windus (2007). How often do Henry James's biographers comment on his no doubt flabby tush?

their own lechery, become armchair, or desk chair, libertines: self-appointed arbiters of (imaginary) female flesh.

Pulling up another example almost at random, just because I read it recently, E. L. Doctorow, an American writer of historical fiction (praised incidentally by Barack Obama, and innocently recommended to me by my own publishers), annoyed me greatly in *The Waterworks*[8] by devoting much attention to his characters' physical attributes. If this is a delaying tactic, it works – it slows everything down to a moribund standstill. The whole book is murky throughout, but every now and then Doctorow rallies to nail someone's outward appearance with strange exactitude. A slave to the habit, he suddenly starts wrestling with the cleavage of the *less attractive* of his two main women characters: Miss Tisdale is a somewhat dowdy counterpart to the saintlike Mrs Pemberton, the requisite stunner (a fixture of much male fiction) who's adored by the narrator and eventually won by his rival in the course of this fitful, circuitous, and unsatisfying book. (I don't think that's a spoiler, since the book's spoiled anyway by all these descriptive passages!) By directing our eyes to the chest of the less hot character, Doctorow magnanimously flings her a little sex appeal, like a bone to a dog:

> Miss Tisdale was petite, but resolute, with a forthright, unaffected manner. Though she was *not a beauty*, she commanded one's attention with her high cheekbones [cheekbones again!] and fair skin and the eyes slightly slanted at the corners, and a melodious voice... She seemed to have no interest in the usual strategies of feminine presentation [tsk, tsk]. She wore

---

8 Penguin (1994).

a plain dark-gray dress, simply cut, with a white collar at the neck. From the collar hung a cameo brooch that rode minute distances, *like a small ship at sea*, as her bosom rose and fell. Her brown hair was parted in the middle and held behind the head with a clasp... *I found her quite fetching*. [my italics]

What is Doctorow getting at with the nautical stuff here, that little ship on troubled waters? Who knows? Male thought is so muddy. After delineating her modest charms, the narrator fesses up to finding Miss Tisdale 'quite fetching'. Kind of him. Without that crumb of forgiveness, Miss Tisdale's sturdy little brooch might well have sunk without trace into the unfathomable depths of Victorian corsetry, in a perfect storm of aesthetic and corporeal deficiency.

Doctorow's approach to Martin, the central *male* figure in the novel, is comparatively lenient. In fact, he gives the guy a godlike superiority:

He was a moody, distracted young fellow... He had light grey eyes which spasmodically widened from the slightest stimulus. His eyebrows would arch and then contract to a frown, and he would seem for a moment to be looking not at the world but into it. He suffered an intensity of awareness — seeming to live at some level *so beyond you* that you felt your own self fading in his presence, you felt your hollowness and fraudulence as a person. [my italics again]

No mention of the teasing glow of Martin's trouser buttons, twinkling like stars, under pressure from his jutting crotch. Nothing like that. Is he even 'handsome'? We don't need to know. Men don't have to be good-looking; they *do* the looking.

So, Martin can flash those light grey eyes of his at us all he wants to. His dignity remains intact. No little boats crawling all over *him*.

～

In her book *Thinking about Women*, my mother Mary Ellmann analysed the sexist stereotypes male literary critics use when discussing women writers:

> Books by women are treated as though they themselves were women, and criticism embarks, at its happiest, upon an intellectual measuring of bust and hips.[9]

If Trump had been a literary critic, this is the kind he would've been. You can almost see him (were he able to *read*) grabbing women by the paperback and sneering at their periods.

My mother noted the way male critics like to identify flaws in women's writing that are curiously similar to the defects men often seem to find in women themselves, such as formlessness, passivity, materiality, and irrationality. Wow. When *men* are the most volatile people around! They steal our power then call us weak, steal our ideas then tell us we're not creative ('Where are all the female composers?' etc.). They stole the EARTH when we weren't watching. And then they dare to tell us we're naggers – when they're *tyrants*.

Nothing much has changed in the fifty years since she wrote her book (except that Norman Mailer has died). Men still equate 'soft body, soft mind', and there are still men who

---

9 Harcourt, Brace & World (1968).

fear that reading a book by a woman is beneath them, and might even deplete their masculinity. Masculinity is such a fragile substance — finite as helium, it's always draining away into the ether. Women like Melania Trump, or even Helen Gurley Brown (who liked to kneel at men's feet), devote themselves to suturing the male ego, but it's a thankless task. In return, men deride, deprive, and misinterpret us. And mansplain. Some system.

My mother said of male reviewers:

When the uterus-mind is seen as conservative or nutritive, it is praised. When it is seen as claustrophobic, it is blamed. By sexual correlation, all energy and enterprise is customarily assigned to male thought, and simple, accretive expectation to female thought. The one breaks through, the other broods. An immobility is attributed to the entire female constitution by analogy with the supposed immobility of the ovum. This imaginative vision of the ovum, like a pop art fried-egg-on-a-plate, is dependent of course upon a happy physiological vagueness. In actuality, each month the ovum undertakes an extraordinary expedition from the ovary through the Fallopian tubes to the uterus, an unseen equivalent of going down the Mississippi on a raft or over Niagara Falls in a barrel. Ordinarily too, the ovum travels singly, like Lewis *or* Clark, in the kind of existential loneliness which Norman Mailer usually admires. One might say that the activity of ova involves a daring and independence absent, in fact, from the activity of spermatozoa, which move in jostling masses, swarming out on signal like a crowd of commuters from the 5:15. The physiological contrast of apathy and enthusiasm might reasonably shift to one of individualism and conformity.

~~~

It will take time to flush away all the stereotypes generated by the Trump era and raise back up all the people he dissed: women, minorities, leftists, outcasts, the sexually and ethnically diverse,[10] the disabled and the poor. What better moment then to hand them the floor, be they chubby, nasty, big-eared, not smart, or a 10, in the overheated estimation of the ex-denigrator-in-chief? At the very least, they'll be a lot more coherent than our unmourned very stable genius.

---

10 This word is now highly suspect, usurped by capitalists. As Angela Davis said, 'Once the word "diversity" entered into the frame, it kind of colonised everything else. All we talk about now is diversity… difference that doesn't make a difference. It's *not* just about diversity, it's about *justice*' (from 'Audre Lorde: A Burst of Light Symposium', March 22, 2014 – https://youtu.be/EpYdfcvYPEQ).

CONSIDER PISTONS
AND PUMPS

We just can't leave the body alone, can we? We really think of little else. It's not just our obsession with looks. Nor our abundant revulsion towards bodily functions and what are generally agreed to be bodily defects, such as obesity, disability, and decrepitude. Never mind all that. What's so bad about *revulsion* anyway? It's a natural and rational state of mind.

No, let's consider the way that we approach just about *anything*, the way that almost everything we do or have or think or want relates to the body.[1] We are surrounded by things constructed to accommodate the human body: cities, cars, furniture, brooms, books, bookcases, hoovers, dishwashers, ovens, cutlery and crockery, pitchers and pictures, toilets and toilettes. Whole lorries travel from Holland full of flowers, just to please our senses (or *used to* before Brexit kicked in).

---

1 'I got my hair, got my head, Got my brains, got my ears...' (Nina Simone, 'Ain't Got No – I Got Life', *Nuff Said*, 1968).

Throughout human history, recipes and clothing fashions have swiftly crossed borders too. We organise ourselves around the body politic, bodies of evidence, bodies of water, government bodies, regulatory bodies, even celestial bodies. Body English! So much BODY stuff going on, it's funny we mostly talk about what's on our MINDS. But but the brain never stops tabulating what's happening in the body.

Linguistically, we refuse to be parted from bodily processes for a *second*. Everything is fucking this or fucking that, or it's shitty, nail-biting, vomitous, stomach-churning, toe-curling, piss-taking, back-breaking, nerve-racking, a pain in the neck, and fit for sore eyes.

We try to stand on our own two feet, put our best foot forward. We're footloose and fancy-free – until we put our foot in it. Meanwhile, our masters, with feet of clay, step on our toes all the time, and bring the down-at-heel to heel. They don't tiptoe around either. And the masses are all ears for their soundbites, until things go belly-up.

These and other coinages like 'eye-watering' or 'down in the mouth' or 'one foot in the grave' show that suffering is a great leveller. That these expressions are ungendered implies an unconscious but kindly craving for sexual equality, a recognition that being *human* may transcend being male or female. When you get right down to it, male and female bodies still have plenty of stuff in common.

But consider pistons and pumps. Shafts, cogs, funnels. 'Male' and 'female' plugs and sockets and computer wires. More than any other part of our anatomy, we equate almost everything with genitalia, and imitate genitalia in the things we make. Our machines are unashamedly coital, just one thing after another either sticking out of something or being thrust into it. And buttons – how we love pressing buttons! It must be some dim collective memory of the G-spot. Every president has to have his or her finger on the Nuclear Button, when they're not buttonholing some underling about losing their shirts.

It's not just guns and missiles that are phallic. In *The Grapes of Wrath*,[2] Steinbeck turns metal farming equipment into something male and malevolent:

> Behind the harrows, the long seeders – twelve curbed iron penes erected in the foundry, orgasms set by gears, raping methodically, raping without passion. ... The land bore under iron, and under iron gradually died...

It's natural enough that we use anatomical analogies. Our thinking sprouts from the sensation of inhabiting a body: you start with yourself and move outward. This habit only gets dicey when the establishment declares one type of body superior to another. Having the *wrong* genitalia (female) currently means exclusion from clubs and other privileges such as respect, encouragement, leadership roles, cultural, economic, and political power, and many dull meetings. It entitles the bearer to *inclusion* in menial tasks, for which women, somehow deemed too frail to become business bigwigs or bullfighters or orchestra conductors, are assumed to have limitless stamina, talent, and patience: tasks involving physical mistreatment and onerous low-paid or unpaid labour. To these, women are expected to add sidelines in cake baking, bill paying, oven cleaning, and eyebrow threading.

---

2 Viking Press (1939). A surprisingly matriarchal novel. The theme of maternal power and heroism peaks in the final image of Rose of Sharon breastfeeding a starving man, reminiscent in its turn of Michelangelo's *Pietà* (which is also, arguably, matriarchal in essence).

The 'inferior' genitalia go publicly unremarked, while the 'superior' genitals are flattered with all kinds of expensive, official, civic homage and imitation (in the form of towers, turrets, plinths, monoliths, etc.). Since Roman times, the phallus has been especially beloved – while nothing about the womb is celebrated at all, except by Judy Chicago and the knitters of pussy hats. This is really rather strange, given that female anatomy has some pretty showstopping faculties (ovulation, menstruation, conception, gestation, parturition, lactation, and mammoth moping). Unless you're a seahorse or octopus, or were born by Caesarean, we all emerge from that juncture where two female limbs meet. The vagina is our red-carpet entrance to the living world. Out we come to seek and find (or not).

In his surrealist autobiographical movie *My Winnipeg*, Guy Maddin gives vulval symbolism a rare weight by repeatedly likening the fork, or Forks, where the Winnipeg's Red River merges with the Assiniboine, to the maternal groin, or 'lap'. At last, a bit of female anatomy hits the big time, symbolically. Rivers make good female emblems, since they flow and brim with life. The Forks is also an ancient meeting point for Indigenous peoples. Many cities besides Winnipeg have been similarly established at the confluence of rivers, for reasons perhaps both vulval and pragmatic. But womanly laps sneak their way into the human consciousness in other ways too, less geological, more literal and abstract: in architecture, in carpentry, in art and textiles; in fissures in stone or the clefts between the branches of trees.

For Robert Frost, forks made all the difference.

So, for a moment let's forget all the impotent phallic symbols so favoured by town planners. The Eiffel Tower can be looked at another way. If you look up its skirts, it becomes a cave, and a monument to the *vagina*. With its legs outspread in a birthing squat, the Eiffel Tower displays its gaping carnal core to the tourists below. As nineteenth-century engineering's equivalent of a cancan girl, it's a flamboyant rival to Rome's Cloaca Maxima. The Eiffel Tower looks like it has girded its loins and expelled the whole of Paris.

Sure, men are cocky now, after all their cockeyed, cocka-mamie cock and bull. The dickheads think they alone have the balls to run the world. Wild ejaculations of respect for testicles spill willy-nilly across the globe. Which brings us to the crotch of the matter: people are rarely acclaimed for having the *breasts* to do something brave, it's always got to be *balls*, cojones – although the grandeur of the scrotal sac, in comparison to breasts, seems highly debatable. In a misogynistic society, one could argue it takes balls to have breasts. As for the vulva, this is only used as a term of abuse. Trump threatened Mike Pence with being seen as a 'pussy' if Pence failed to (illegally) overturn the results of the 2020 election: 'You can either go down in history as a patriot, or you can go down in history as a pussy.'[3] Well, what else is new? They're both assholes.

Haven't we had enough seminal insights too? Men are always having those. They avidly disseminate their seminal ideas, in fact set such great store by anything seminal that they sometimes ascribe seminal achievements to women too. The obsession with *balls* persists, while all the fabulous, life-enhancing, life-generating wonderments of ovaries, Fallopian tubes, placentas, clitorises, labia, both minora *and* majora, are ignored. Where are the ululations for the uterus, the catchphrases of the snatch,

---

3 'Pence Reached His Limit With Trump. It Wasn't Pretty', *New York Times* (January 12, 2021).

the wit of the slit, in recognition of the crucially productive female groin, lap, funnel, box, spoon and fork? This really gets on my tits. But soon female germinations will be nursed to maturity, through a new fluidity of thought – if we could just egg on female supremacy a bit.

The ceaseless avoidance of vulval symbols is nuts. Let's return to the womb – you know you want to. It's time society was more womb-based. In honour of our new age of free tampons, we need to discharge a heavy flow of labial lingo and symbolism across the land, along with some hot flashes of vaginal ideology. As our emblem, the Statue of Liberty, with her multitudinous motherliness.[4] Mother Nature, Mother Hubbard, Mother Goose, mother love, mother vinegar, mother-of-pearl, the mother tongue of the motherland... The 'Mother of Exiles' was eulogised by Emma Lazarus, who awarded her an attitude very foreign to our bully-boy times:

> *Give me your tired, your poor,*
> *Your huddled masses yearning to breathe free,*
> *The wretched refuse of your teeming shore,*
> *Send these, the homeless, tempest-tost, to me,*
> *I lift my lamp beside the golden door!*

The gal has a lamp, because motherhood is an *enlightening force.* That's why, when your mother fades, darkness falls.

Motherhood has always been a moral force for good, and proof of women's importance in the world, whatever men might wish to believe. If most of human history was, as I suspect, matriarchal, human society was originally founded on

---

4 Built coincidentally with the help of Gustave Eiffel.

the exertions of the womb. Birth was a risky but honourable undertaking in prehistory, and women were cherished and respected, not just as potential mothers but *for their own sake.* What a revolutionary idea. Not repressed, not raped. *Respected.* Now women are paid less and violated more, and the female body has been ghettoised, strong-armed by machismo.

Time to put feminine curves back into the body politic. It's so flat without them! Pence, who calls his own *wife* 'Mother' (an Oedipal mix-up not to be encouraged), got all tangled up over womb contents a few years back when he was governor of Indiana, endorsing an abortion law so extreme that it required all foetal remains to be reported to the government and formally cremated or buried. Noting that their every discharge was now apparently of intense interest to Mike Pence, some women decided to keep him informed of every stage of their menstrual cycle. They heaped him with daily updates on flow, spotting, cramps; and included Trump, once Pence was chosen as his running mate in 2016. This uterine barrage only ended when Twitter suspended the @periodsforpence account. But briefly, the menstrual taboo, which requires women to keep totally shtum all their lives about their periods, and also about the lack of them (menopause), was demolished.

Well, it's a start. But we could get more mileage out of female naughty bits than that. We need city councils and cartographers to reclaim the matriarchal world order, inch by inch, with feminising place names. The hell with those little hamlets, Rump and Penice. We need: Womanhattan, Wombburrow, Wombledon, Breechbourne, Breastworthy, Tittsburg, Clitoropolis, Oviductia, Fallopidelphia, Loudmouth, Womenhoe, Uxoriousbridge, and the twin cities of Multiple and Orgasm. America already has the Carolinas, Louise-iana, Georgia, Virginia, and Mary-land.

Let's restore Petticoat Junction, and the adjacent Hooterville. In Britain, there's Maidenhead, Maidstone, Bournemouth, East-bourne, Westbourne, Winterborne, Wombwell, Womenswold, Wigglesworth, Witchford, Titford, Thrushelton, Pity Me, Wendy, The Wash, and Crackpot. It's a start.

And we'll always have Lapland. Next stop, the Milky Way (breast is best). Now, I don't expect a standing *ova*-tion for this plan. Just let it gestate – it's pregnant with possibilities.

THE WOMAN
OF THE HOUSE

It's all so innocent: you live in a log cabin with the guy you love, snuggle up every night under your home-made patchwork quilts, churn butter, tend animals, bake bread, gather water, milk cows, sweep the floors, beat the rugs, black the stove, regularly refill mattresses with fresh straw, cook stuff, sew stuff, mend stuff, make mock apple pie out of green pumpkins, slap bears on the back (thinking they're cows), never ever forget to do the dishes, and somehow give birth, all alone, to any number of helpful children. That's the woman's point of view.

The man's? You perform powerfully outdoors: you hunt, you fish, you farm, you trade furs and news at the general store, and head home afterwards despite blizzards, buffalo wolves, bears, more bears, and tree stumps that *look* like bears in the dark. Your gun is slow, you think before you shoot, you examine unfamiliar migrating birds with interest, you help anybody you see in difficulty, and you can rustle up a little log cabin any old time. And a well to go with it! In the evenings, after a sturdy meal of bacon, lard, biscuits, and gravy, you either whittle a trinket shelf or take out your fiddle and sing.

A far cry from the state of the union today, in which the woman works full-time, worries constantly about calories, celebrities and cellulite, and routinely does ninety-eight per cent of the housework while the husband holds down *two* jobs or none at all and spends his leisure hours assessing porn. The kids go to school, where they are gradually indoctrinated into a society that cherishes men, money, and misinformation over the measliest little bundle of human rights.

All of this was in train when Laura Ingalls Wilder's family wandered the American plains in their covered wagon – they just didn't know it yet. They thought the further west you got, the freer you would be. Or Wilder's father did anyway. He had a bad case of wanderlust; his wife had more reservations about the pioneering life. Neither believed America, founded on usurpation, desperation, the forlorn ideals of misled emigrants, and the confused philanthropy of forefathers, had been stitched up from the start. But who helps you in a capitalist society when the locusts eat your crops, or fire destroys your homestead, or the bank calls in your loan? Kin, *if you're lucky*, and maybe your neighbours. Mostly, you're on your own – because everybody else is too busy and confused trying to *comply* with capitalism to think of outsmarting it. In *The Grapes of Wrath*, the inequities shine out clear as day. There's only so much anyone else can do for you, however compassionate they may be. If you help each other *too* much, it strikes of communism, a total no-no in the eyes of most Americans. This is a nation that eats propaganda for breakfast.

They should all have stayed in Europe! (Wilder's mother had Scottish ancestry, and her father English). Still, it's nice to assume, even wrongly, that things might go well. Charles Ingalls, depicted as 'Pa' in the *Little House* books, had a gift for keeping cheerful. When things were tough, he sang his 'trouble song' and got even happier. Here's the deal: you kill, you cook, you eat, you teach, you build, you repair things, you tend your livestock, you hitch up the team, you save lives when need be, and you do it all with a positive attitude or *you're all going to die*. This is one of the few situations in which optimism is not a sign of imbecility but a necessity. Or at any rate, it sure comes in handy. Cynicism can slow you down.

The Ingallses' impoverishment is at times severe, but they ride it out with impressive courage and good humour. One winter, Pa has to walk hundreds of miles, in worn-out boots and a thin coat, to find enough work to keep the family alive. On an earlier excursion, he's blown off course in a blizzard and has to hole up in a snow cave for three days, subsisting on the few pieces of Christmas candy he was bringing home to his girls. This is Depression literature, as was *The Grapes of Wrath*. When Wilder began publishing these childhood memoirs in the early thirties, Americans were in all kinds of trouble. They knew what she was talking about. And in the current fallout from Covid, Brexit, and a cascade of global financial crises, the Ingalls' hardships, economy measures, nomadism and other survival tactics sadly have a renewed relevance.

∿

Her clued-up daughter, the writer and journalist Rose Wilder Lane, warned Wilder there was no market for children's fiction. But, in need of money, Laura pressed on and between 1932 and 1943 produced a big hit, her eight-volume series of autobiographical novels. Beginning with *Little House in the Big Woods*, set in Wisconsin, the books, based on Wilder's experiences as a child, were aimed at a young audience. They're adventure stories but also catalogue her absorption in nature and the domestic realm. They illustrate the female side of the Western Expansion, and follow a family triumphing against tremendous odds to retain a way of life that incorporated play, music, education, and kindness. Not a bad way to live, on the whole.

Yes, there are troubling blunders and omissions: the chapter on the minstrel play, for which Wilder's father wore blackface, is unbearable to read. It is now a chastening record of a tributary of racism that for some time people regarded as merely light-hearted pranks: dressing up as African Americans. And Wilder is not sympathetic enough toward Native Americans either. She's hardly cognisant of them. She isn't callous, exactly – leave that to Betty MacDonald in *The Egg and I* (1945). MacDonald never stops bad-mouthing in the bitterest of terms all the Indians she encountered during her own Western adventure (at the age of twenty, she married the first bloke that came along, and to her surprise he wanted to live on a farm). Macdonald speaks more highly of the local drunks! Wilder, on the contrary, had a humility and innate morality that saved her from outright bigotry. She even admits to some shame about the treaty betrayals, abuse, genocide and displacement of Native Americans that were taking place around her as a child.

She has a refreshingly pragmatic attitude to the idea of America too, that is never overly obsequious or smug – a respectable stance in a country that has now gone belly-up under the weight of self-styled patriots. Wilder could tell an ignoramus when she saw one. She was not unaware of Native Americans, nor intolerant of them, but had very little contact with them. So, compared to MacDonald's obnoxious hostility, Wilder's occasional hesitancy on the subject seems fairly mild for the times. A pity that in her first book, she myopically claimed their little house in the Big Woods was far from *any other people*, when in fact many Native Americans lived nearby. She also treats her mother's distaste for Native Americans as a legitimate point of view, though Wilder herself isn't sold on it. Jack the faithful bulldog is: he was so antagonistic towards Indigenous Americans that he became a liability. When the family built a cabin – illegally – in Indian Territory, Jack had to be tied up a lot so he wouldn't make trouble.

Wilder mentions in *By the Shores of Silver Lake* that *white* men slaughtered all the wild buffalo (on which Native Americans depended). So she's somewhat aware of the sins of colonialism, and disapproves. In one of the later books, *These Happy Golden Years* (1943), Laura (Wilder's authorial custom is to speak of herself in the Third Person) and her future husband Almanzo (or Manly, as she called him), a young farmer from De Smet, ponder an old Indian mound they discover when out courting in a horse buggy. These are clearly not the most racist people around: they don't rush to *desecrate* the mound at least, as many less enquiring people were always doing.

The takeover of the American continent is relatively recent, conducted over the last five hundred years or so. But the *myth* of America as a pristine and primordial land lingers in American minds, especially during childhood. When out walking alone as a kid in a Chicago suburb, I often imagined myself either as a giant scaling mountains in a single bound (not sure where I got that idea), or as a *pioneer* traipsing through the wilderness, brave and free, in search of the right spot to build a cabin. The latter fantasy was probably Wilder's fault, and may explain her continued popularity. Who doesn't wish there was territory still left to explore, and land there for the taking? (Poor Mars.)

Laura Ingalls Wilder was not the problem; *Christopher Columbus* was, and reparations are not enough. The American 'experiment', now over, needs to dispose of itself in an equitable manner. Time to give the whole place back to the indigenous peoples and ex-slaves who suffered there the most, and see if *they* can fix it.

⌇

Now that people are ruthlessly scolded for failings in youthfulness, health, and wealth, Wilder's modest, non-judgmental and practical world view (reinforced by Garth Williams's illustrations from the 1950s) seems strikingly humane, even *socialist* at times. Despite the family's isolation, the *Little House* series becomes a tribute to community spirit. That is now an outmoded and radical notion in the United States, but America could not have come into being without collective effort. In *Little House on the Prairie*, Ma *overcomes* her antipathy to Native Americans enough to feed the Osages who own the land the Ingallses mistakenly occupy, and her hospitality is rewarded: the chief later saves them all from slaughter.

The Ingallses are especially charitable towards fellow settlers, tirelessly, even *tiresomely* so: I still don't get why Laura has to give her beloved rag doll to that spoiled neighbour kid, Anna Nelson (don't worry – Laura steals it back a few pages later). And there's the moment when, after slaving away all day and night for the church fund supper and never getting a morsel to eat herself, Ma seems to lose it for once and actually glares at Pa, who's babbling about how well the whole thing's gone.

But it's in *The Long Winter* that communal duty really triumphs. The inhabitants of De Smet, marooned for seven months by snow, and beyond the reach of the trains on which they depend for coal and food, have begun to starve. Every few days brings another ferocious three-day blizzard in which it's dangerous to leave the house at all. Two teenagers, Almanzo Wilder and Cap Garland, selflessly make a hazardous forty-mile round trip in search of some rumoured bushels of seed wheat on a stranger's claim. By chance, from seeing a wisp of smoke from his chimney, they manage to locate the guy in his dugout, bargain for the wheat, bag it up, and lug it arduously back to town just before the next deadly blizzard hits. The greedy capitalistic storekeeper then tries to sell this hard-won wheat for a profit to the desperate townsfolk. The customers get ornery, threatening to steal the wheat instead, until Pa persuades the storekeeper to think again. (Pa, Charles Ingalls, is often the hero in these stories – when it's not Laura herself.) *He* calls his solution to the problem 'justice', not socialism, but the storekeeper's mercantile mercilessness collapses under the power of Pa's argument, and everybody gets enough wheat to survive. It's really a very anti-American solution.

～

Both parents are strict at times. Pa (Charles) comes across as the more charismatic of the two. When excited about anything, it's to him that Laura goes. Ma (Caroline) is a little less welcoming. She's steady, orderly, perhaps shy (like her daughters), and usually compliant and subordinate. She has some influence, but only occasionally exercises it to stop Charles doing something reckless. Her restrained, somewhat pious personality is softened for us by Pa's evident pleasure in her: their love sustains them and keeps the whole family alive. At one point, he climbs off the roof of the house he's building, just to hug Ma. He frequently praises her domestic know-how and 'Scottish' frugality, and her cooking drives him wild – 'Ma always could beat the nation cooking.' When their food runs low, he says the imprint of Ma's palm on the cornbread is all he needs. (Now all we have is palm oil, in everything! Acquired through child labour, while orangutans die.)

Wilder's world is full of work of the female hand. These stories aren't just about woods and prairies and creeks: they're about the *house* in the woods, the *dugout* by the creek. Wilderness is there, they believed, to be tamed by the American family, and this particular American family is almost wholly female. According to these recollections of Wilder's, pioneering was rarely a solo masculine activity. *Somebody* had to knit the socks, produce the babies, and make the codfish gravy to go with all the cod philosophy. It takes guts to cross the frozen Mississippi in a covered wagon, with your children huddled in the back. Ma even helped build the cabins, injuring her foot once in the process. And the spring cleaning is simply beyond belief.

Once settled somewhere, women imposed *home comforts* on the cabin, essential to survival. It's Caroline who figures out that they can grind wheat with the coffee mill during the long hard winter, to make the bread that is their only nourishment. It's she who brings literature into their lives too – Tennyson, no less – and insists the children go to school. There might well have been no *Little House* books without Ma's respect for education. She's also responsible for the braided rag rugs (which she teaches the girls how to make), the hair receivers (these things sound terrifying, but apparently they were much treasured objects in which to store lost hairs taken from a comb or brush, so as *eventually* to make, unbelievably, a pincushion or some other curio – it's a free country, I guess), their death-defying long underwear (itchy red flannel), all the cooking, pickling and preserving, and supervising the family's individual Saturday night baths (a big palaver). The domestic chore Laura hates most is sewing – she'd rather be outside helping Pa with the hay.

> Sewing made Laura feel like flying to pieces. She wanted to scream. The back of her neck ached and the thread twisted and knotted. She had to pick out almost as many stitches as she put in.

Nobody knows what feminism is any more, but it isn't just about equal pay and abortion rights. It's about appreciating femaleness for femaleness's sake. Wilder, who notably refused to say she would 'obey' Almanzo during their wedding ceremony (a conversation she inserted, for good measure, into one of her books), never elaborates on the source of her feminist bent, but it may stem from some awareness of her mother's strength. Wilder was much more rebellious herself, as seen in the fictional Laura's many moments of dissatisfaction and indignation, the sisterly rivalry (she admits she often wants to slap her older sister Mary), her physical courage (she saves her little sister from wolves and blizzards, endures a two-month stay with a knife-wielding madwoman, and was an enthusiastic rider of unbroken horses, bareback), her curiosity (while Mary stays indoors like a good girl, Laura's out playing in the snow, or peeking at men building a railroad), and the occasional naughty escapade (such as luring Nellie Oleson into a leech-infested pond). All in all, Laura's quite a bold role model for little girls.

⌇

Practically silent as a writer until her sixty-fifth year, apart from a poultry column in the local Missouri paper, Wilder suddenly delivered this touching account of settler life from a female perspective. Taking nineteenth-century individualism to include *herself*, Wilder daringly, and without apology, wrote about the daily lives of women and girls. Most of their activities are dutiful enough, of course. It was a restrictive world, in which bustles really mattered, lace had to be crocheted, and hoop skirts got stuck in doorways or invaded by kittens. At puberty, you put your hair up and lowered your hems and began to notice your family's stony broke. Wilder didn't rebel against any of that, but she did approach difficulties with an admirable sturdiness that belied her shyness.

She is at her best describing her *own* childhood as a frontier girl, but her second novel, a one-off, was about a boy: *Farmer Boy*. This tribute to her husband Manly (Almanzo Wilder) was based on his early life on his parents' thriving farm in Upper New York State. Though clearly an act of love, the book sometimes descends into envy. Wilder dwells exhaustively and pretty yearningly on the quite startling amount of food on offer in the New York Wilders' household. Pancakes, sausage cakes, golden buckwheat cakes, gravy, oatmeal, thick cream, maple syrup, fried potatoes, preserves, jams, jellies, doughnuts, spicy apple pie: that was breakfast. For snacks during the day, Manly got apples, doughnuts, cookies, popcorn, and watermelons. For supper: four large helpings of fried apples 'n' onions, roast beef and brown gravy, mashed potatoes, creamed onions, boiled turnips, 'countless slices of buttered bread with crab-apple jelly', and, for dessert, huckleberry pie, blueberry pudding, and a thick slice of birds' nest pudding covered with sweetened cream.

At Christmas things got even grander: roast goose and suckling pig, candied carrots, cream pie, mince pie, horehound candy, and fruit cake. But even an ordinary Sunday for Almanzo's family involved a three-chicken pie, beans, and 'fat pork' (bacon?), accompanied by pickled beets and rye 'n' injun bread, followed by pumpkin pie. Oh, and why not a piece of apple pie with cheese to go with that? This was all provided punctually by Manly's dexterous, hoop-skirted mama – while the Ingallses feasted on blackbirds, if they were lucky, and they were grateful for the occasional rabbit, pat of butter, or salt on their potatoes.

But wait a minute – how does she *do* it, Almanzo's mother? I find it hard enough to feed two people *once in a while* – how can there be all these mashed potatoes and doughnuts everywhere, when the woman has no servants and is usually to be found huddled upstairs over her loom, weaving huge bolts of woollen cloth for the suits she sews for her husband and numerous sons? Or else she's spinning, dyeing, knitting, patching, darning, churning her prize-winning butter, and making a year's worth of candles. She makes her own soap too! The only thing she *doesn't* do is card wool: it gets machine-carded in town. What a slugabed. Sheesh, lady, get real.

But the whole family works hard. When not partaking of dishes fit for a king, the nine-year-old Manly worked like a dog outdoors – weeding, baling, shocking, ploughing, planting, sowing, hoeing, harrowing, hauling, mauling, heaving whole logs around and chunks of ice, and breaking oxen and horses all by himself. The Wilders were engaged in a constant frenzy of back-breaking bounty and industry.

～

'Have to finish my mother's goddam juvenile,' wrote Laura's daughter Rose, referring dismally to the latest children's fiction manuscript Wilder had sent her. Rose Wilder Lane's substantial role in the *Little House* editing process has unsettled some Laura fans. A feminist and activist (first a communist, then an early libertarian and very anti-FDR), Rose was a well-connected writer who really got around: when she wasn't babysitting for her friends Sinclair Lewis and Dorothy Thompson, she was travelling the world, adopting Albanian kids, or taking off on road trips around America with John Patric or Zora Neale Hurston. She wrote freewheeling biographies of Charlie Chaplin, Jack London, and Cher Ami, the heroic WWI homing pigeon (Chaplin sued; Jack London's widow objected vehemently; Cher Ami made no comment). Lane also produced a few (adult) novels of frontier life, borrowing a lot of her mother's material: grasshoppers, debt, wolves, etc. *Let the Hurricane Roar* (1933), published the same year as Wilder's *Farmer Boy*, is a novella full of struggle and cataclysm that, in the absence of the heartfelt quality of her mother's 'juveniles', smells of the lamp. Lane lacks her mother's connection to the lived pioneer experience. Still, her books sold so well that her fame wasn't surpassed by Wilder's until some time later.

Wilder didn't envy her daughter's literary career at all, from what she gleaned of it during visits. She once commented in a letter to Manly, 'the more I see of how Rose works the better satisfied I am to raise chickens.' But after financial disasters hit the whole family, partly due to Rose's bad investment ideas, she encouraged her mother to get writing, which was the only way Rose knew how to make money. Lane's biographer William Holtz has implied that Lane proceeded to turn her mother's mud into gold.[1] But *Wilder's* biographer John E. Miller vetoes this interpretation of things.[2] His view is that Lane's contribution to the *Little House* series was less rewriting or ghostwriting, as Lane herself called it (she did ghost for Herbert Hoover), as thorough line edits, questions, coaching, prodding, pressurising, squeezing, and some light censorship. Plus a lot of bossy advice. So, more typing and griping than magical transformation. Miller convincingly establishes Wilder's dominant role in a working arrangement that was always fraught, with many disagreements on content that Wilder usually won: she was a toughie.

Writing is a process of loosening up, unravelling what has been balled up tight, an abandonment of silence and abbreviation. Lane helped draw her mother out, but may never have fully grasped what her mother went on to accomplish. Knowing something, though, about the children's book market, when she could Lane steered Wilder away from venturing into dark subjects, including illness and death. Wilder snuck some hardships past her, though. She refused to leave out her older sister Mary's blindness, for one, claiming that this event changed everything for the family and had to be there. She was right: the books would have less life to them without that tragedy and the fluctuating relationship between Laura and Mary.

Lane didn't manage to remove every *peculiarity* in her mother's writing either. Wilder's technical descriptions – of

---

1 *The Ghost in the Little House* (University of Missouri Press, 1993).
2 *Becoming Laura Ingalls Wilder* (University of Missouri Press, 1998).

how to construct bobsleds, railways, whatnots, extremely complicated Victorian dresses, or grow a giant milk-fed pumpkin – can be very hard to follow. Undaunted, she often interrupts the progress of the story to explain, say, how Pa made a door-latch (I guess, just in case you're ever lost in the wilderness yourself). It's a bit like getting a bookcase from IKEA:

> First he hewed a short, thick piece of oak. From one side of this, in the middle, he cut a wide, deep notch. He pegged this stick to the inside of the door, up and down near the edge. He put the notched side against the door, so that the notch made a little slot. Then he hewed and whittled a longer, smaller stick…

Uh huh? 'Up and down near the edge', you say? Right. Wilder's also got quite a bad little comma habit, and uses the word 'little' a little too much. If Lane was hoping for a more sophisticated literary style from her mother, she lost that battle from the start. The writing remains flawed, limited, and often very plain. But it has its charm.

〜

Maybe Wilder just needed more practice. The writing grows up with its readers. The early books are a bit thin but by the time she produced *On the Banks of Plum Creek*, Wilder was getting into her stride, with more emotional depth, more drama, better character development, and a wistful attention to landscape – cattle out of control, flooding creeks, locusts, sunsets, that sort of thing. As customary in survival stories, there is a steady supply of ill fortune: Mary's blindness, the harsh winter (the true horrors of which *were* softened to placate Lane and the publisher), the family's occasionally acute penury, and their efforts to overcome it. But there are also genuine delights: music, singing, sleighing, rolling down an irresistible haystack, getting a fur cape for Christmas, and the poignant moment when they're sitting around the campfire on their trek west, fearing Jack the bulldog has drowned in a flooding river. But he *turns up*, creeping cautiously towards them in the dark.[3] Big relief for the reader.

The older Laura gets, the more she emerges as a fully conscious being, both naughty and inventive – qualities that come in handy when she exacts her leech revenge on her nemesis Nellie. Her impatience with churchgoing, too, is frankly put:

> Laura thought [the preacher] would never stop talking. She looked through the open windows at butterflies going where they pleased. She watched the grasses blowing in the wind... She looked at her blue hair ribbons. She looked at each of her finger nails and admired how the fingers of her hands would fit together... like the corner of a log house... Her legs ached from dangling still.

Religion is torture, but hardly anybody in America will admit it! Wilder stuck ostensibly with conventional Christianity, but late in life admitted her *joie de vivre* really came from a naturalist, even pagan, bent:

> I can still plainly see the grass and the trees and the path winding ahead, flecked with sunshine and shadow and the

---

3 Jack's death scene later on was all made up. His actual end is unknown – they gave him away. Jack, Jack! Poor racist dog.

beautiful gold-hearted daisies scattered all along the way.
I am beginning to learn that it is the sweet, simple things
of life which are the real ones after all.[4]

Throughout the books, memories of such things are meaning-
ful to her and lush, and it's in these pastoral recollections of
the outdoor world that Wilder's at her most elegiac. But who
are these descriptions for? Surely not *kids*. They assume more
feeling for meadows, birds, and flowers than I think most urban
children ever had. As a child, I skipped them. Now I like them.
Maybe she just wrote these passages for *herself*, to record and
revisit sensations that mattered to her.

Another crucial element in the books is Laura's fondness for
her father, who can converse with birds on the violin:

Phoebe-birds called sadly from the woods down by the
creek... Softly Pa's fiddle sang in the starlight... The large,
bright stars hung down from the sky. Lower and lower they
came, quivering with music... The night was full of music,
and Laura was sure that part of it came from the great, bright
stars swinging so low above the prairie.

Yes, her frequent mention of stars can get aggravating – especially now that we can't see any at all. (I couldn't even see the
recent conjunction of Jupiter and Saturn. Bah.) But on a *prairie*,
stars count for something.

The whole family likes a joke. When the government forces
them to move on at one stage, like Steinbeck's Joads, leaving
the house they'd effortfully built with their own bare hands (all

---

4 From the *Missouri Ruralist*, 1917 (quoted in Miller, *Becoming Laura Ingalls Wilder*).

except for the precious store-bought glass windows), Pa claims they're actually taking away more than they'd brought with them.

'I don't know what,' Ma replies.

'Why, there's the mule!' Pa says. The horse he'd spent their last few pennies on had unexpectedly given birth to a mule. But they've got something else as well, something equally stubborn: the girl in the back of the wagon, taking it all in.

THE LOST ART OF
STAYING PUT

Not that long ago, air travel was a badge of distinction. The jet set prided itself on the habit, and Sinatra sang 'Come Fly With Me' to encourage them further. Mile-high sex on a plane was de rigueur and considered only slightly less point-scoring than surviving a hijack. People actually used to dress up to take a plane (*before* getting naked in the lavatories). Pan Am claimed '*The travail has been taken out of travel*'. For some, the excitement still lingers. One blogger, in the rarefied world of airline fandom, flew himself and his wife from Houston to Frankfurt, just to try out United's new Business Class perks. 'This flight was also special,' he enthused, 'because my wife... would become a United Million Miler. I can think of worse ways to celebrate.' I can't.

You'd think the joy of flying a million miles on a plane would be over by now for most people, especially since the advent of Covid (long plane rides being just about the most perfect way to catch and carry it'). But apparently people still miss flying. During the early days of Covid, some diehard would-be travellers visited Taiwan's locked-down airport just to experience the sheer thrill of going through Security and wandering the departure lounge: fake checking-in, fake passport control, fake luggage screening, fake duty-free shopping, fake airplane, fake flight attendants. People signed up for this! They didn't fly *anywhere*. Incredibly, these fanatics were really missing the whole airport experience.[2]

Nostalgia for trains, yes, I can understand that, but airplanes? Modern flying is about as stimulating as filling out tax forms, and Covid makes it crummier yet. A global pandemic could reasonably be an opportunity to reconsider the whole crazy business of zooming about the globe like this, but instead loads of people are itching to jump on board again as soon as it's allowed, and egging others on to do the same. Less for the pleasure of flying perhaps, or even of vacationing, than that of exciting the customary envy in friends and colleagues by temporarily depositing one's pallid frame on a foreign beach. In the midst of the pandemic, the *Sunday Telegraph* urged people to 'hop around the Pacific... wander with reindeer in Russia... take the kids to Tajikistan... track big cats in Mongolia... connect with nature in Australia... [and] spend the summer hols in Namibia'.[3] Uh no, don't, please don't.

---

1 'In 2019, the HHS [Dept. of Health and Human Services] conducted Crimson Contagion, a simulation examining the government's ability to contain a pandemic... The scenario envisioned an international group of tourists visiting China who become infected with a novel influenza and spread it worldwide' (Lawrence Wright, 'The Plague Year', *New Yorker*, December 28, 2020).

2 Aditya Singh hung out in Chicago's O'Hare airport for three months, apparently for fear of Covid. You've got to really like airports to do that. ('Man lived inside O'Hare for 3 months before detection...', *Chicago Tribune*, January 17, 2021.)

3 December 27, 2021. What'll the newspapers *do* if people stop booking these needless trips? All that ad revenue down the drain! No. Commerce outweighs Covid and the climate crisis.

Travel is now such a habit, people just can't imagine life without these regular culture-shocking transplantations. They risk death, disease, penury, language barriers, and bedbugs (who wants BEDBUGS?), not exactly to 'find themselves', but to find themselves in a new time zone. Do they think it's actually *time travel*? The famous, and not so famous, often *die* just getting someplace they believe they have to go: Carrie Fisher, Glenn Miller, Helen E. Hokinson, James Dean, Buddy Holly, Bessie Smith, Albert Camus... These sobering examples seem to deter no one. And then there's Robert Frost, for ever debating that tricky dilemma in the woods:

> *I took the one less travelled by,*
> *And that has made all the difference.*

How about taking *neither* road, bub? Ever thought of *that*?

〜

Everybody's mindlessly weight-watching and whale-watching these days, in individual acts of migration that echo and often accentuate their addiction to individualised transport, the car. But, as the Covid lockdowns have proven, we don't absolutely have to drive everywhere, we don't each have to own a car.

When I first came to Britain in the 70s, not everyone had a car. A significant number of middle-class men never learnt to drive, preferring to be driven around by others. I drove a few of those guys around myself. Mistake. But now people act like owning a car is a wholly justifiable necessity, just something adults do. They object to fatal motorway crashes only when they cause *traffic jams*. Nobody seems to notice what a terrific waste of *time* it is to drive yourself about in a tin can. They never question having to spend a tenth of their lives in furious, anxious, high-alert situations, negotiating their own individual, cumbersome, smelly, expensive, lethal death box-on-wheels round every-one else's individual, cumbersome, smelly, expensive, lethal death box-on-wheels. The parking, the licensing, insuring, and tax-discing, the servicing, washing, polishing, and valeting, the vandalism, car theft, and carjacking, the skids, the crashes, the scratches, the close calls, the roadkill, road rage, the AA, the RACs, fluctuating petrol prices, three-point turns, black ice, bird shit on the windscreen, the embarrassment of not knowing how to check the oil or fix a flat tyre, the scary purchase of the car in the first place, and (worst of all) the snoozefest of having to read a *car manual.* How do they endure all this zooming and blinking and passing and honking and emergency braking and power steering and satnav, and the buzzing, the buzzing!

The noise of motorways has by now ruined many a rural idyll. Yet, as Covid has proven, most drivers don't really need to commute to work at all, nor see every friend or enemy in person all the time. We have Zoom, and Zoom backgrounds, and Zoom cat filters, for that. We have BOOKS too. Books on travel – these could save you a trip. You don't *have* to see the seven wonders of the world, you know, nor visit geographically distant family members. Even if, oddly, you *want* to see them, you can in fact survive without each other (which is why you live so far apart in the first place). No need to fly around the globe to attend football matches either – cardboard fans can do that for you now (one could argue the fans were cardboard *before*, along with their robotic excitement). So, why all this dumb transporting of our vulnerable bodies from place to place, at the expense of our nerves, our sanity, our health, our time, our bank balances, and the environment? New York's champion and wit Fran Lebowitz, who claims she has a carbon *fingerprint*, not footprint, only travels for work. For pleasure, she stays at home.

> As far as wanting to go places, I can't believe people do it for fun. When I'm in airports and I see that there are people going on vacations, I think, how horrible could your life be? Like, how bad is your regular life that you think: you know what would be fun? Let's get the kids, go to the airport... with these thousands of pieces of luggage, stand in these lines, be yelled at by a bunch of morons, leave late, be squished all together – and this is better than their actual life?[4]

*

Airlines ought to have Jerk of the Year awards, and not just for the passengers but for their own employees. These days, you need a bulletproof vest just to deal with the cabin crew. It's awful that United's planes proved attractive to jihadists – 9/11 was the most sorrowful tragedy to hit America since Vietnam and as a result of it, United's staff must still be under constant strain. But so are the passengers! *They're* tired of terrorism too, of having to queue to take their shoes and belts off, of cramming shampoo into 100ml bottles, of forgetting their small change in the Security trays and having their favourite nail scissors confiscated – only to be met essentially by bouncers once they reach the plane, uniformed despots who ban ten-year-olds for wearing 'inappropriate attire' ('form-fitting' Spandex leggings)

---

4 'Metropolitan Transit', *Pretend It's a City* (directed by Martin Scorsese, 2021).

and bully a mother of twins for bringing a pushchair aboard.[5] Airlines now actively hate on their passengers. If they can't bump you off the manifest just by yelling at you, next thing you know you're bodily kicked out of the plane. On a Hawaii to LA flight, Delta recruited airport police to threaten a couple with jail and the *confiscation of their children*, merely for refusing to give up a seat they'd booked and paid for.

Airports and airlines seem very exacting about how passengers behave. They make you wander miles of shops, starve you, bore you, intoxicate you, hassle you, despise you, and then pillory you for your resultant 'air rage'. More and more passengers do threaten to shoot everybody or leave the plane mid-flight. Some complain about sitting next to fat people, or start eating their own mobile phones as a form of protest. In disaster movies, pilots wrestle with the yoke, trying to get full throttle — now they just throttle the yokels.[6]

United has a particularly high rate of animal deaths.[7] United allegedly killed Simon, one of the largest rabbits in the world. Poor Simon. And it was a United flight attendant who forced a woman to put her ten-month-old puppy in the overhead locker, where it smothered to death during the flight.[8] Pups and rabbits

---

5 'After Barring Girls For Leggings…' (*New York Times*, March 26, 2017); 'American Airlines Suspends Flight Attendant After Altercation Over Stroller' (*New York Times*, April 22, 2017).

6 Airlines never stop squawking about Covid travel restrictions ('UK aviation sector need urgent support, industry leaders say', *Guardian*, January 16, 2021). What crybabies, after they helped spread it everywhere in the first place!

7 'In 2017, United had the highest number of animal deaths of any US carrier… with 18 animals killed and 13 injured in transport. Six animal deaths in total were reported from the other 16 carriers…' (*Guardian*, March 14, 2018).

8 'United Airlines "saddened" by death of giant rabbit after transatlantic flight' (*Guardian*, April 26, 2017); and 'Dog Dies after United Airlines Attendant Forces It into Overhead Bin' (*Independent*, March 13, 2018).

go quietly belly-up, Spandex-clad teenyboppers sob and slip back into obscurity, taking their improper contours with them. But the sight, in 2017, of the tactics used against Dr Dao on a United Chicago to Louisville flight, provoked lasting outrage. The airline had apparently overbooked the flight, as they frequently do. A legitimate ticket holder, with patients to see the next day, Dao declined requests to give up his seat. As a result, he was eventually dragged by force, bleeding, half-conscious and half-naked, off of the plane, in front of all the other passengers. He was left with a broken nose, a concussion, and two lost teeth.

Originally from Vietnam, Dao said the experience was more horrifying than the fall of Saigon. United's CEO, who defined his staff's violent approach as 're-accommodating' people,[9] and unconvincingly described Dao as 'disruptive and belligerent', had to perform some pretty tricky manoeuvres to steer the airline out of its self-inflicted PR nosedive. But even he couldn't censor all the new slogans:

> *United: putting the hospital back into hospitality.*
> *Fly the unfriendly skies.*
> *Red eye and black eye flights available.*
> *Board as a doctor, leave as a patient.*
> *If we can't seat you, we beat you.*

Dao's plight resonated because it encapsulates the now customary destruction of human dignity and the will to live, otherwise

---

9 'I apologise for having to re-accommodate these customers' (https://hub.united.com/response-united-express-3411-2353955749.html; https://eu.courier-journal.com/story/news/2017/04/11/male-hs-teacher-aboard-united-flight-didnt-need-happen/100319308/; and 'United's Apologies: A Timeline', *New York Times*, April 14, 2017).

known as air travel in the twenty-first century. Next time they ask if there's a doctor on the plane, will anyone reply?[10]

But okay, let's say you aren't machine-gunned, beheaded or hacked to pieces with a machete on your way to so-called Security. Let's say you survive the invasive (radioactive?) full-body scan, as well as the obligatory two-to-three-hour Duty-Free dwalm in the departure area. Let's go crazy and suppose you make it to your seat on the plane without being publicly shamed or socked in the jaw, either by airline staff or the people sitting near you. Your reward is that you now must *fly*.

During the cramped, airless, comfortless journey that follows (for which more and more wondrously you have to *pay*), amid air contaminated by engine oil and the pesticides used in fumigating the plane, a martyr to the airline's idea of water, alcohol, snacks, and movies, you will also be at risk of congestion, constipation, nausea, dizziness, headaches, hypoxia, jet lag, deep vein thrombosis, solar flares, fleas, pandemics, colds, flu, flatulence, and whooping cough. No one ever seems to voluntarily delay a flight because of illness, even Covid-19 – that would be cowardly. No, they tramp on board in service to their microbes, and cough, sniff, and exude contaminants all over you for hours on end. You can catch Ebola or TB in the time it takes you to untangle your gratis audio set.

I'm not saying your seat is small, but if it were a haystack, you'd find the needle. While the business-class swells chow down

---

10 Flight attendants somewhat redeemed themselves in January 2021 by urging their union to establish No Fly lists banning Trump's supporters from homeward-bound planes after they'd staged the coup at the Capitol. ('Flight Attendants Call for Pro-Trump Rioters to be Added to the No Fly List', *Revolt*, January 11, 2021.) That was heroic, and the surprise this move caused amongst the insurrectionists was pretty gratifying.

on their business-class lunches in their business-class lounges at the airport, and, once on board, guzzle their business-class suppers, encased in their big-assed business-class thrones, making big-ass business-class deals and getting business-class grease from their business-class filets mignons all over the business-class upholstery, the *Economy* passengers' food, if it ever arrives, is a throwback to TV dinners of the 1960s. Or maybe they *are* TV dinners from the 1960s? I once ordered the kosher meal, just to see if it was any more palatable. The stewardess unceremoniously (and, I thought, rather antisemitically) flung a solid block of ice labelled 'KOSHER' on to my tray table. Inside it you could dimly see some kishkes. It might have thawed by the time we reached Patagonia, but I wasn't going to Patagonia.

⌇

I have no objection here to purposeful uses of travel, of course, as in the case of emergency workers, international election monitors, refugees, or political, economic, or environmental migrants. Seeking a safe haven is a human right and unavoidable amid war, injustice, and climate change. It's also beneficial to the host society: as Fran Lebowitz said when discussing New York City, 'Immigrants make the culture and tourists ruin it.'[11] So, though travel's no picnic, let the nomads, grape harvesters, sheep shearers, job seekers, asylum seekers, detainees, gypsies, adventurers, artists, earthquake sniffer dogs, and St Bernards with their little casks of brandy go wherever they need to go. My beef is with frivolous travel of the selfish kind, the act of

---

11 'Who's Afraid of Fran Lebowitz?', All About Women Festival, March 6, 2018 (Sydney Opera House Talks and Ideas Archive).

inflicting yourself, uninvited, on other cultures, this constant movement to and fro of the chronically rich, with their taster menus of destinations to which they're attracted purely due to their own lack of direction, humility, and self-knowledge.

In winter, weather forecasters often warn people to avoid anything but essential travel. The trouble is, whenever anybody hears this, they seem to leap *immediately* into their cars and get caught in snowstorms. Maybe it was the same paradoxical impulse that led the Prime Minister's senior advisor Dominic Cummings, at the start of England's first lockdown in April 2020, to drive his whole family (some of them, including Cummings, already displaying Covid symptoms) from London to County Durham, including an educational side trip to Barnard Castle. His excuse for the latter jaunt was that he needed to test his eyesight. There seems vast disparity in determining what 'essential travel' is.

Is *any* travel really essential though? I understand that *some* travel is a necessary evil. Hoover salesmen and drug dealers have to keep on the move. Ditto estate agents, reporters, imams. It's *leisure* travel, the time-filling, culture-sampling, cuisine-dissing, planet-defiling, water-guzzling invasions of the overprivileged that I really abhor, and that unthinking, knee-jerk rush to the computer to book cheap flights every January (we barely even notice we're doing it any more!) because without a gad-about in Guadalajara, a dubious spree in Dubai, or the chance to go berserk (over pea soup) in Zeebrugge, people apparently lose all standing in society. We could just stay home and listen to Scarlatti but no, people are bombarded with bucket lists of faraway things they *must* accomplish, and they fall for it! Lambing in Maine, prancing through Croatian lavender fields, pottering round the Pyramids, personally inspecting the coral reefs and rainforests before they are no more (thanks to all the people who flew out to see them), riding on a donkey, a dromedary, a double-decker, trotting through Central Park in an anachronistic open carriage (who *does* that?). A hot dog here, couscous there, sashimi up, tortellini down, *Figaro su, Figaro giu*, always seeking some remnant – any will do – of uniqueness and authenticity in a world the human race is racing to destroy. *Figaro, Figaro, Figaro!*

We're such saps. We've been fed a great big bunch of flimsy reasons to travel, by evil geniuses determined to use up all the oil and gas as fast as possible so as to coerce us into adopting 'cheap' nuclear power, a craven idea that will torment and baffle future generations for thousands of years to come (if there *are* any future generations). Do we ever stop to think about all this motion, this *commotion*, this agitation and all of its attendant aggravation? Far from it. We gullibly galumph across the earth at our masters' bidding and get ourselves into all kinds of scrapes. We get lost, we get robbed, we get raped, we get fleeced, we get flummoxed, we get misdirected, mistranslated, and misunderstood, we get hot, we get cold, we get sick, we get nervous, we get confused. We get delayed interminably in airports. We unwisely hang off cliffs or drown in waterfalls, all for the sake of a selfie. We struggle with unfamiliar phones, plumbing, and foreign currency, and collect bottles of limoncello or artichoke brandy, just so we can hold our heads up high when we finally limp home sick, broke, exhausted and bewildered.

Aviation accounts for 3.5% of global warming.[12] The effects of cement production are far worse, I'm told. Yes, okay, there's too much cement. But 3.5% is not nothing. And cement is

---

12 Hannah Ritchie, 'Climate Change and Flying' (ourworldindata.org, Oct. 22, 2020).

probably more lastingly useful to people than the obligatory Mediterranean swim, New Zealand cider tasting, or yet another Thanksgiving with the aged p's. But we continue to prioritise human mobility and interaction over all other considerations, even despite the current plague. Meanwhile, the Great Barrier Reef dies for us. It's lost half its corals in the last twenty-five years and is eighty per cent bleached already, cooked alive.

Birds are allowed to migrate without too much human inter-ference and their flights don't cause global warming. Officially though, only *people* are now free to dart all over the place. We let passengers with Covid cross borders all the time, but the Australian government got all worked up about the arrival in Melbourne of a racing pigeon who seemed 'foreign'. Joe the Pigeon (named by the man who first spotted him) was consid-ered a potential biohazard because he might have been carrying an American pigeon disease. Joe was therefore in imminent danger of being euthanised or deported. But later it was decided he was Australian after all.[13] It's *people* who should undergo this sort of rigmarole – not euthanised perhaps, but banned from travel.

Animals bear the brunt of our allegiance to travel, and not just in the effects of global warming on wildlife. We now inflict travel on animals themselves, from the meat industry's horrific live animal transport operation to the way day-old chicks and exotic pets are mailed around the world. Then there are the doomed personal encounters with animals when on holiday. Ever tried to save a stray cat or a mistreated dog in some foreign country? It's not easy – they don't have passports. No, your trip is much more likely to *damage* a local animal. A young sniffer

---

13 'Fake US leg band gets pigeon a reprieve…' (Associated Press, January 15, 2021).

dog was shot dead at Auckland airport in New Zealand in 2017, just for capering around loose at the airport and delaying a few flights. He wasn't even on the tarmac, but in some outer perimeter area. Birds, being a danger to airplane engines, are routinely shot or poisoned in the vicinity of airports. All for 'your travelling comfort'. This is what you unwittingly commit to when boarding a plane, the possibility that animals will be executed in honour of your pointless itinerary – and not just the ones they make into 'selected medallions of beef'.

Donkeys get the worst of it, but they're getting wise to us. According to Olga Tokarczuk, Jordanian donkeys now baulk at having to carry American tourists around. They don't want to be ridden by Americans, Americans are too obese.

> The donkey is an intelligent animal, it can evaluate weight right away, and it will often start to get upset just seeing them come off their tour bus, all overheated, big sweat stains on their shirts, and those trousers they wear that only reach their knees.[14]

In Santorini, waves of Americans pour off cruise ships in hopes of finding a horse or donkey to take them up the hill. Many animals have been injured coping with this onslaught.[15] No wonder donkeys start to bray and buck when they see Americans closing in on them. (Don't we all?) One of the better things about Covid has been the thought of Paris *free* of American tourists: their weirdly compulsive descent on that city has been briefly halted.

---

14 *Flights* (tr. Jennifer Croft, Fitzcarraldo Editions, 2017, p. 125).
15 'Tourists urged to avoid riding donkeys up Santorini's steep steps' (*Guardian*, April 2, 2019).

There are Americans who will not visit anywhere in Europe that doesn't have a Holiday Inn. There are Americans who spend their whole time in England disputing the British pronunciation of Birmingham. There are Americans who refuse to enter Ely Cathedral on the grounds that Britain has not yet sufficiently recognised America's part in winning the Second World War. (Actually, America had a lot of help.) And there are American children who can detect insurmountable differences between Scottish McDonald's and New Jersey McDonald's. There is an American blind spot to other cultures that really gets in the way of their deriving any discernible benefit from travel. *So why go?* Be content to stay in Birmingham, Michigan, gobbling your Happy Meals.

Americans scour Bulgaria for a whisky sour. They freak out if their credit cards don't work, or the plumbing's weak, the bandwidth too narrow. They fall in the lousy limey hotel shower, break some bone, and to their utter disbelief get X-rayed and bandaged at the hospital for free. (Yes, it's called socialism.) Everywhere they go, they assume and *insist* that everything is or should be done the American way; otherwise it's weird. They assume everybody knows English – if they don't, they're weird. Everything *amazes* them, everything comes as a great big shock. You mean this was built before the *American Revolution?* Gee. You mean I have to put some of these crazy coins into this *slot* and then the bus will take me where I want to go? Weird. And, having almost single-handedly caused global warming, the way Americans freak out about rain seems rather overplayed.

The Accidental Tourist,[16] the most biting of Anne Tyler's customarily timid and meandering novels, hits the nail on the head regarding the insistence of many American travellers on

---

16 Knopf (1985).

remaining completely unaffected by the places they visit. 'Other travellers hoped to discover distinctive local wines; Macon's readers searched for pasteurized and homogenized milk.' Trump's a good example of this type of tourist, taking his own steak and golf clubs with him everywhere he goes. He takes his whole dull family too! Or the ones he acknowledges as family.

~~~

In the seemingly endless American TV series *Away*, a recent Covid-binge-watch from Netflix,[17] five supposedly multinational astronauts (the Commander's American, the other four are foreign but *act* American) head off for Mars together in what must be the worst-made space rocket of all time. Something is always going wrong with that ship! But there's really very little about space travel or astronomy or even about Mars in the show. Instead, the drama is entirely taken up with crying and trembling, the exchange of potent glances amongst the crew, and messages of love with people on earth – people whom, let's face it, the crew has just *determinedly* left behind. But boy do they love and love and LOVE them. It's exhausting. The humourless commander (Hilary Swank) is an emotional wreck throughout the trip. I wouldn't let her drive a little red wagon. Yet here she is, steering her own space capsule towards Mars along with her four homesick minions, each of them an anxious, emaciated pin cushion of platitudes.

Their bodies are spontaneously *decomposing* before their eyes because of weightlessness, there's a big water shortage due to the ship's lousy plumbing, and there's the constant danger of death

---

17 Created by Andrew Hinderaker and aired in 2020.

from all those pesky unforeseen consequences that tend to crop up when one's a million miles from home (and oxygen). But still, like American travellers everywhere, they all remain absolutely unchanged and untouched by anything that happens to them. Even a year-long trip into outer space leaves them cold. What *is* the point of Americans going anywhere? Especially Mars, of all places – that's a lot of love miles, and an expensive traipse through the solar system, so far from hot dogs and the Super Bowl, while again and again and AGAIN, they phone and email and record declarations of devotion for their boring families in case they die. How they cry. (Wasting water!) Someone in the script department failed to heed Frank Capra's advice, that it's the *audience* who should cry, not the actors.

～

Travel is colonialism. Travel is WAR. Religion travels fast, as does ideology. Tourists, missionaries and our roving billionaires pretend they mean well but they don't. They haven't come to help, they've come to take advantage. The Romans really got around too. You'd think taking hot then tepid then cold baths, eating dormice with fellow aristos in Rome, and running around on pretty mosaic floors to the chimes of your tintinnabuli, with the occasional outing to Pompeii for an orgy, would be enough for anyone. But no, Roman generals were always on the move, subduing, crucifying, enslaving and decimating people, paying centurions in salt, importing wheat, papyrus, grapes and gossip, and building walls to make Rome great again. The trouble is, when you're away from home too much, things go to pot and, if you're not careful, you come back to find it's not only your colosseum that's cracking but your whole civilisation.

The movement of people and ideas, grandly called globalisation and exemplified by the Columbian exchange,[18] is not just an innocent sharing of cultures and silk trading. Columbus, along with his overt sadism, managed inadvertently to transport to the 'New World' worms, rats, smallpox, chickenpox, typhus, scarlet fever, leprosy, malaria, whooping cough, gonorrhoea, TB, and the bubonic plague. He picked up potatoes, tobacco, and syphilis on his way out. A real import-export kind of guy, he unified the world with mutual catastrophes. Thanks a bunch. Since then, international interaction has led to industrial horror, wars, slave labour, the spread of kudzu and Dutch elm disease, pandemics, a regrettable cultural homogeneity and oceans full of plastic. The pretence that going global might spread wealth and strengthen ties has proven hard to buttress, with trade wars and people starving just outside the five-star resort precincts to which wealthy travellers dumbly flock.

All anyone gets out of this passing acquaintance with foreign lands is a crushing conformism, an expensive revitalisation of arrogance, and the obtusest form of worldliness, wherein they blindly experience the same banalities the world over: the same slang, same pop music, same video games, same crummy hotel decor, same fast food, same views of Notre Dame, same big wheels, same terrorist atrocities, same jogging trails. Travel *kills* as much knowledge, taste, and culture as it purportedly spreads. The compulsion for sameness has an insidious effect: languages, costume, dialects, and accents start to die out as soon as the Coke and jeans and T-shirts arrive. To ensure uniformity and reduce the chance that the traveller will actually experience something new, major cities now offer exactly the same chain

---

18 Alfred W. Crosby, Jr., *The Columbian Exchange* (Greenwood, 1972).

hotels, restaurants, and designer stores – ideal receptacles for morons on the move. But if Prada, Superdry, and H&M are *everywhere*, what's the point of city-hopping shopping?

Cuisines travel invisibly between countries, and English cooking was radically improved by French influences (even in the midst of the Napoleonic wars), and later by Indian flavours and recipes. It's arguable that the shameless British takeover of India is all that's made it possible for today's British food-ies to *survive* (chicken tikka masala is now the UK's national dish). But is it really necessary for rivalrous *marmaladers* to circumnavigate the planet, flying all the way from Australia to Lake Windermere to show off their marmalade at a marmalade festival? Marmalade. Yes, it's hard to make a good one. But must we burn the last of the fossil fuels just to prove it can be done in *Australia*? (Which I still doubt.) Funny kind of conserve-ation that is, and a world away from Elizabeth Bennet's hopes for her planned trip to the Lakes:

> Oh! What hours of transport we shall spend! And when we *do* return, it shall not be like other travellers, without being able to give one accurate idea of anything. We *will* know where we have gone – we *will* recollect what we have seen. Lakes, mountains, and rivers, shall not be jumbled together in our imaginations; nor, when we attempt to describe any particular scene, will we begin quarrelling about its relative situation. Let *our* first effusions be less insupportable than those of the generality of travellers.[19]

---

19 *Pride and Prejudice* (1813). As it turns out, she goes to Derbyshire instead and spends most of the trip thinking about Darcy.

Woody Allen's best work is long past,[20] but his film-making in his dotage slid even further downhill once he started setting his bottom-drawer scenarios in Destination Cities. Most European capitals now exist merely as theme parks for this kind of cinematic abuse (Jason Bourne leaves them in *ruins*), along with their function as bachelorette party, beer binge, and corny lover hotspots. Prague, Dublin, London, and Barcelona have been drained of meaning and individuality, and are now completely interchangeable.

Edinburgh, where I live, used to be a fine old mirthless town, grim, austere, dirty, and dignified. Twenty-first-century marketers have turned it into a fairground. Whenever possible, the city's few green spaces get trashed by amusement arcades, glühwein, vomit, festivals, fringe festivals, markets, fringe markets, outdoor exhibitions and exhibitionists, coffee bars, beer tents, merry-go-rounds, tat stalls and ice-skating rinks. The pavements are falling to pieces, the parks and trees are in a state of collapse, the trash is never collected, and the lockdown puppy poop is never scooped. The homeless used to die on the streets while the Edinburgh International Festival conducted its annual month-long experiment in overpopulation and over-pricing. The fireworks displays alone used to be relentless, *daily* in August. Occasionally there were wee calls from residents for *silent* fireworks, but their requests couldn't be heard over the din.

This historic city, once home to the Scottish Enlightenment, has been intentionally emptied of thought and refilled with fake fun. Edinburgh has reinvented itself by obliterating its own

---

20 As the Martians tell him in *Stardust Memories* (1980), 'We like your movies, particularly the early, funny ones.'

inventiveness. Writers get short shrift: Burns, Boswell, Henry Cockburn, David Hume, James Hogg, Walter Scott, Robert Louis Stevenson, Conan Doyle, Muriel Spark, and even Irvine Welsh wouldn't know the place. All we've got now is J. K. Rowling and Alexander McCall Smith, the Betty Boop and Mickey Mouse of Scottish letters.

~~~

But you simply must see the Taj Mahal, pussycat, or Machu Picchu, or Outer Mongolia, before you *peg out*, we're told again and again and *again*. All exotic places *must* be trampled. *Immediately*. It torments people to think of leaving a single foreign banquette unwarmed. Just mention the Galapagos or the Faroe Islands and watch them jump – because they've got to get there before everyone else. Before it's *ruined*. The seagrass meadows of the oceans are disappearing at the rate of *two football fields an hour* just so people can boast about having bothered a turtle in some unfortunate clime.

The truth is you *don't* personally have to survey every square inch on earth, no matter what your so-called friends tell you or what you read in all that newspaper and magazine travel porn. After all, the only really interesting thing about travel is seeing new flora and fauna, and we've killed off most of that. What is more important in the end than listening to Bach or reading Dickens? *Humankind should be your business*, not this hypnotic holidaying. Locusts are big adherents of bucket lists too; they too strive to get out and about before they die.

But no, we must endorse every work break, school break, birthday, death, divorce, bicycle accident, cancer remission, basketball game and gender reveal party with a long, hazardous flight or drive to somewhere or other. There are a million family occasions that require your presence (we act like we still live in villages and the bris or grindingly dull graduation ceremony is only a block away!), a million new reasons to travel are manufactured every moment. Grief, joy, honour, guilt, humility, curiosity, habit, tradition – all can be met by a remote pageant, banquet, fair, hot tub orgy, or jamboree.

Courses for this, courses for that. You can, you *must*, attend a week of weaving, and probably weeping, in Wales; a five-day workshop making doll's-house furniture in Cumbria; a backgammon cruise through the Norwegian fjords; courses in hillwalking, pottery, juggling, watercolour, yoga, I Ching, karate, quinoa cookery, or the arrangement of spit curls, in a compound situated anywhere from Padstow to Phuket. How does a crash course in straw-hat manufacture, drystane walling or Orkney laddering grab you? Or why not discover lost tribes in the Amazon, then lose them again; or learn sock-knitting in the Arran Isles, croissant-twirling in Dieppe, asparagus farming, wildflower and mushroom differentiation, or even scything. Yes, there are classes in scything. What they need is a creative *writhing* course.

You can do a restaurant crawl through sub-Saharan Africa, or put a poor old pony through its paces all over Iceland. Almost simultaneously, if you must. Tired of London and Londoners? You can solve this by flying all the way to Montana on an unsuccessful 'man-hunt' and write an article about it for the *Spectator*, turning innocent strangers into props for your fantasy life. Sex and travel often merge this way: it's not called a 'drive' for nothing. Many travellers hope a change of latitude will cure their sexual lassitude. Can't they just put on a French accent and *pretend*? No. Passion requires the sacrifice of fossil fuel.

The more blatant sex tourists, the ones with nothing to declare but their criminality, incessantly cross the globe, sharing their diseases and disillusionment with the young and desperate of other countries. The Grand Tours of Europe – nicely encapsulated by Laurence Sterne, who liked to be 'incontestably in France'[21] – were open excuses for debauchery. Sterne may well be the *only* novelist who should ever have been allowed to travel. Apart from Joyce and Wilde, that is – it's essential for Irish writers to leave Ireland.

Gun shows, pedigree cockapoo summits, koan contests, horse races, guru reunions, nirvana attempts, stag shooting, Bayreuth pilgrimages, and gangster get-togethers where they plot assassinations, offload stolen jewellery, and swap nuclear materials, are further great reasons to travel. Spark up your plastic surgery experience by getting it done in Mexico, Moscow, Bulgaria, Beijing. Lipo on the lido! Visit chateaux, Chartres, shacks, shepherd huts; wineries, cattle farms, tobacco plantations, roller coasters, and wildlife refuges. Gaze on every sort of bull torture. Climb various famous groups of mountain peaks. Tour Cézanne's studio. (If you'd turned up when he was *alive* he'd have killed you.)

How about a nice artist residency? All artists now have to travel. They'd probably rather be paid to stay home, where they're already set up with a studio, assistants, and paint-bomb machines. But no, the whole world's watching and it's hard to resist the pressure, the prizes, the prestige. You're nothing as an artist these days unless you've spent a month in New Mexico, the Arctic, Trinidad, Tibet, and Sumatra, and regularly attend the Venice Biennale. People forget that reality is *wherever you*

---

21 *A Sentimental Journey through France and Italy* (1768).

are. It's what you're thinking about that matters, but nobody cares about that. Anyway, everybody's thoughts are so scattered now — because of the jet lag.

People travel for business. Until Covid struck, academics *never* sat still — they were constantly in the air overhead, deconstructing something. Rewarded by financial bonuses and promotions for business trips and abstruse conferences, and ordered not to return without some impact and relevance, people learn to crave these junkets and to crow about how many they've been on. Their underlying assumption is that travel is irrefutably fun, worthwhile, and enviable — a status symbol — when really all that's happened is that these poor wretches (more sheep than locusts, and therefore to be pitied) have left their work and their lives behind in order to spend twenty-eight hours in the air and in airports feeling disoriented, twelve hours drinking in a variety of unsanitary places, an hour or two at a dull meeting or under-attended talk, and a few hours playing hooky in unfamiliar surroundings and getting laid by a drunk and equally lonely business colleague, assistant professor, or total stranger. The possibility of sexual shenanigans, such as they are, is the big draw.

～

Eco-tourism is a nebulous concept, whereby the deteriorating environment is further warmed and eroded so that people who think they really *understand* nature can go enjoy its last gasps by surfing it, scuba-diving it, or climbing, caressing, and collecting it. The world's tiniest begonia, newly discovered in Peru, is now at risk of being *squished* by a million amateur botanists stampeding up the hill in a frenzy to mark it off their score sheets. Nature would be much obliged actually if we would just LEAVE IT ALONE.[22]

There's a multitude of alternative health tourism too, ashrams, hot springs and sulphur spas, meditation camps with ley lines to lie on, curative meccas to heal you in some short-lived way. You know what? Making debilitated people feel duty-bound to go to Lourdes, Baden-Baden, the Grand Canyon, the Dead Sea, or the Swiss Alps for the sake of their health is one hell of a despicable idea.

Alternatively, for those who have it all and want *less*, there are staycations, essentially stagnations, where you still spend a lot of money on yourself but stay within a few hundred miles of home patting yourself on the back for 'saving the planet'.[23] Or how about a *starvation* vacation, where you go all the way to Bavaria for a toxins purge, releasing *more* toxins into the atmosphere in your wake for the *rest of us* to purge, in a self-perpetuating contamination cycle. It's a capitalist's dream come true: pollute the whole world by detoxifying *yourself*.

'Groundhog holidays' are for unadventurous vacation-*repeaters* who want to return to the same dump in, say, Cancun, or Majorca, or the Black Sea, *anywhere*, even Denver, year after year. Well, you part-own some hideous condo so you've got to go at least once a year to make sure all the ashtrays are just where you left them. People really do this, and kick up a fuss if the other fifty families they time-share with have moved a chair!

---

22 As soon as humans desert a place, 'feral eco-systems' emerge, no-man zones much appreciated by wildlife. See Cal Flyn, *Islands of Abandonment* (William Collins, 2021). Kim Stanley Robinson recommends leaving *half* the earth free of humans (*Guardian*, March 20, 2018).

23 The *planet* will survive actually, whatever we do. But *we* won't. *We'll* be extinct. And what a shameful mess we'll leave behind. Dinosaurs and giant sharks lasted millions of years, and left the place as they found it.

These scaredy-cats are a world away from the daredevil traveller, the climbers and hotheads and perilous sports advocates.
Skiers fly thousands of miles just to put themselves in traction.
Arctic aficionados, jungle johnnies, rhino poachers: the idea is
to test yourself and return home euphoric for having survived –
if you do. One minute you're in Texas, the next you're up Everest
in a blizzard, on a trip that set you back $100,000. They can't
help it, risk-taking is addictive. There are so many mountain-
eers trying to 'summit' on Everest right now, they really ought
to install a funicular. In the movie *Everest*,[24] a whole group of
semi-experienced climbers gets caught on some narrow ledges
without gloves or even a sleeping bag. It's hard to believe, and
harder to watch. (What I hate most is the way they all pretend
to be interested in Nepal.)

Maybe the real purpose of travel is to scare yourself.
First, on the plane (or other speeding vehicle), and later, at
your sunstroke-ridden, malaria-swamped, typhoon-prone,
elephant-stampeded destination. It's all an experiment in
alienation, a stranger danger endurance test. People really
can't decide between the horror of staying at home and that
of dying in transit. They replace their natural fear of travel
with *fear travel*, travel designed to scare you a bit. What is a
trip to Vegas for after all but to *frighten* yourself by excessive
drinking, whoring, and gambling? The birds do it, the bees
do it, the holier-than-thou jihadists do it, and everybody likes
Tom Jones.

〜

---

24 Directed by Baltasar Kormákur (2015).

You don't *have* to poo and pee and copulate and take snapshots of well-known landmarks in every country on earth, you know? It's not the law. But the PRIDE travel engenders is beyond belief. Smugness is a guaranteed travel bonus: they hand it out during take-off and landing.

I go [someplace], therefore I can gloat.

We booked, we bustled, we boasted.

Maybe people got sick of Marco Polo's reminiscences too, and of Vasco da Gama's, and greeted Amerigo Vespucci's cocktail party chat with heavy sighs and glares – 'Guy's been to Rio twice and never shuts up!' But at least travel then involved some genuine challenges. Now there's very little to be proud of – if you have the dough, you can get pretty much any place you want, and fast. So, what's with all the triumphalism? 'We've been to China,' they coo, or (the lesser claim), 'We haven't been to China *yet* but we're going to go.' China's old hat! Everybody's been to China now, even vegetarians (who always complain about the food – so why not stay home and eat your *own* damn bean sprouts?). Once they've done China, they have to top that with something even more exotic – Guatemala, Micronesia, the moon. Okay, go if you must, but don't come back.

And they're so bossy, these modern-day explorers, especially if you travel together. Having been somewhere once for a *week*, they're bursting with superior knowledge of the place. They alone now know how to find the lesser-known museums, or what to order in Marseille (bouillabaisse) or Oaxaca (a tamal). They tramp you all over Moscow without pausing for a pepper vodka. They know every hidden lily pond in Lagos or Lisbon, and where to find a dentist, from Clapham to Cape Town, but they don't know when to go fly a kite and jump in the lake.

The reckless needlessness of most travel is never touched upon by these eager beavers. Instead, we're all just automatically supposed to join the exodus, at the risk of stability, sanity, and solvency. The illogicality of this push to be on the move is nicely touched on by Padgett Powell in *You & Me*, when two sedentary characters consider taking a supposedly desirable trip from Florida to some desert – a plan which actually fills them both with dread. None the less, they try to convince themselves to go.

> Our tiny growing familiarity alone, as we sit there or walk around parched and frightened, will convince us we now know more than we did before the onset of the fear and the disgust, and we will feel better about the desert.
>
> Veterans of an hour in the desert, we will like it, a little bit.[25]

*

Even charitable or political-action tourism can fall flat. It was great, for instance, that women marched on Washington to protest during Trump's inauguration in 2017. Brava! But it would have been even better if they'd *walked* all the way instead of flying. And once they got there, why not *stay*? If only they'd camped out on the White House lawn until their wishes were met. Until the guy gave up the presidency in shame. But of course he has no shame.

---

25 Echo Press (2012).

However heartfelt the expedition is, the means almost always defeats the ends. Apart from those kind ophthalmologists who fly around Africa or Haiti fixing cataracts (hoorah!), and maybe a few UN or Peace Corps employees here and there (hard to verify), it's time to reconsider most forms of supposedly altruistic travel. You might do more good in the world if you quit with the wanderlust and sent the cash you save to somebody who hasn't *got* any disposable income. The *New York Times'* educational trips for high school students, in the company of *Times* journalists, cost $5,000. On one such Student Journey to Peru, the kids were apparently 'taught' racism and disdain for the concept of white privilege.[26] *The Nation* offers similarly priced trips to Cuba for adults, as if there were something extra responsible about gadding about in a country America tried to boycott out of existence. These olive-branch tourists would presumably never dream of sacrificing five thousand bucks each to *help* Cuba or Peru directly.

Another popular destination for the conscience-stricken is the European concentration-camp circuit. Great day out for all the family![27] The Nazis put fossil fuels to previously unimaginable uses, and you too can deplete what remains of our irreplaceable energy supply by transporting yourself – voluntarily! – to Auschwitz to gawp at the gas chambers in a Hawaiian shirt.

The biggest travellers, the wealthy and mobile twenty per cent, are causing the most environmental damage. As Bob Hughes observed in his book about the ways in which technological liberation has liberated *nobody*, bikes and even horses

---

26 'Star NY Times Reporter Accused of Using "N-Word"...' (*The Daily Beast*, January 28, 2021.)
27 Sergei Loznitsa has covered this new type of voyeuristic jaunt in his movie *Austerlitz* (2016).

are not only cleaner forms of transport but *quicker* too, if you calculate the actual time and energy invested.[28] Airlines claim that their ever-bigger aircraft are more egalitarian and environmentally friendly, but they never add in the costs of enlarging runways, building the planes, and hiring enough Security goons to flatten all the passengers – I mean, protect passenger safety. There's nothing admirable about getting on an Airbus.

∿

As for the VIRUS, what *it* likes are cars, restaurants, airports, globalism, poverty, superspreader get-togethers, close contact, coughing, panting, yelling, and a catastrophically diminished environment. Covid *loves* to travel and it really gets around. It thrives on apathy – ours and that of our lethargic and asinine leaders. Let's thwart it, beef up what the virus *hates*: community, quiet, carefulness, consideration, stasis, solitude. Clean air. Masks. Morality. Conservation, the common good, individual commitment to a single locale. And *staying put*. We fight it with *these* while we wait for the vaccine, whaddya say?

The UK's Covid lockdown in the spring of 2020 did have one heartening effect: an almost instantaneous burst of wildlife. Birds sang more – for once, they could hear each other. Plants seemed to grow more vigorously, with better air and no one outside to trim or trample them. Weeds blossomed boisterously. Streets were calm and quiet. For a little while in Edinburgh, we were spared the sight and sound of cars in motion, and even of tourists clanking their wheeled suitcases over the cobblestones.

---

28 *The Bleeding Edge: Why Technology Turns Toxic in an Unequal World* (New Internationalist, 2018).

Dolphins have been spotted in Venice. In Hong Kong, within a week of the cancellation of the usual two hundred express ferries to Macau, native dolphins returned in great numbers. They played in the water, and apparently had lots of sex. Dolphins really know how to live – if only we'd let them.

There is beauty in less activity, less financial transaction, less mayhem, less hurry, less frenzy, less movement.

Individuals are *not* responsible for global warming, it's true. Corporations are largely to blame. But irresponsible individuals don't help! Maybe what we need is an intervention: just put travel addicts on a low-mileage diet, or make them go cold turkey. If they need ongoing support, they can join Carboniferous Anonymous (CA), a twelve-step programme I just made up for people stuck on burning up all the fossil fuels.

It will be hard to stick to your resolve at first, especially when you see your friends scoring their usual peregrination points. You may even be shunned for not putting yourself through several long-haul flights a year, not catching the usual half a dozen colds, and not knowing the best coastal bus route in Honolulu (No. 55). Don't listen to them. Sticks and stones will break your bones, but travel buffs will never hurt you. Throw out your cholera pills. Recycle all those little plastic toiletry containers. And try having sex with people who live nearby.

BRAS:

A LIFE SENTENCE

It's like always meeting under a PYLON. The bra is the omni-present structure of the twentieth century and now the twenty-first. Every woman you know, love, hate, help, vex, need, revile, misconstrue, and repudiate is probably wearing one, has worn one, and will continue to wear one every day of her life. Aunts, mothers, grandmas, teachers, doctors, estate agents, travel agents, theatrical agents, secret agents, dental psychiatrists, friends, sisters, daughters, and nieces are all enduring this unmentioned bondage, post-puberty, and we just accept it! They live and DIE in bras. Stifling cups and biting straps and niggly hooks and rotting elastic and silly little bows and frills and embroidered flowers or polka dots. Women have come and gone, fledged in love and hope and doomed to desolation, all whilst wearing bras. Their upper torsos have been twisted, tainted, squeezed, and adulterated by these garments, which rarely make them happy.

MEN HAVE MANAGED TO EROTICISE BRAS, BUT THEY DON'T HAVE TO WEAR THEM.

Apparently the smooth back of the human female must never be seen; it can only appear in public, roped in, with seams criss-crossing it, and bulges along the seams, that are now more familiar than a real breast, unleashed. We are so offended by the rocking and rolling of breasts when loose, so ignorant of their natural substance and behaviour, we have reached the delusional state of thinking it unnecessary and *outlandish* that breasts should ever wobble at all. Their gelatinous quality will not do. In its place, we get engineering feats that are more like BRIDGES than breasts. Are we trying to get to the other side?

CHILDREN MUST WONDER IF BREASTS WOULD *FALL OFF* IF THEY WEREN'T FASTENED ON BY BRAS.

Women survive WARS, or don't, wearing bras. They cook thousands of meals wearing bras. They have arguments, go to movies and restaurants, go to the DOGS, wearing bras. They even manage to BREASTFEED wearing bras. They drive, they run, they dance, they trip, they fall... some even try to sleep, wearing bras. They collect prizes, pensions, the kids, the gro-ceries, and the service wash, wearing bras (and have to wash the damn things back home *by hand*). They're badgered by authorities and family members, beaten by bad men, given parking tickets, and disallowed child custody, wearing bras. They're kept so busy doing all that stuff, they don't have time to OBJECT to bras. Ideally, they'd be offered *tax-free handouts* annually, in compensation for this sartorial torment. Instead, all they get are strong shoulders, from toting their breasts in bra baskets all their lives. Only during the politically advanced sixties and seventies – and in 2020, as a vegging-out by-product of Covid lockdowns – have there been some poignant efforts at bra-avoidance.

MARILYN MONROE NEVER TOOK HER BRA OFF.

Considering the physical responsiveness, sensitivity, and the erogenous tissue of what it encloses, the bra is pointedly anti-sensual. It pulls, it pierces, it pinches; it exerts a death grip all day. It causes rashes, chafing, irritation (both mental and physical), and lasting striations on the skin. And form follows function: the bigger the breasts, the uglier the bra. Apart from the lace (if you're *lucky*), most bras are made of very weird materials, unbecomingly combined. Policing the breasts is the main requirement. The topographical complexity of the territory and elaborate design standards also ensure that bras can never be home-made, so manufacturers can change whatever they want for these straitjackets. Compared to the authoritarianism of these compulsory fabric containers, breasts begin to seem primitive, rudimentary, RUDE, idle, anarchic, whimsical and unschooled. Unstrictured structures, ripe for rebellion, breasts are dubious, naughty, irrelevant, optional, a subject of debate, practically ILLEGAL. Breasts are *detainees* – tracked, branded, interrogated, maligned, discouraged, and 'supported'. No other body part suffers from this level of scrutiny and distrust.

THE STRAPS CAN BE SNAPPED BY
GOOFBALLS
TO ADD STING TO RIDICULE

Breasts have clearly seen their day. Shabby and outmoded, their future is bleak. With the help of implants, they've even started to EXPLODE. This makes wearing a bra yet more vital, as protection for others in the vicinity. Mayhem might ensue if breasts were ever released from their prisons, so there they stay, serving life sentences, and our compliance is chilling.

MORNING
ROUTINE GIRLS

How convenient for capitalism that the self morphed so easily into the cell phone. The doomed and the dying use selfie sticks to record their every car accident and tiger encounter. The Web is awash with self-promotion, from glossy offerings like *Comedians in Cars Getting Coffee* (in which Jerry Seinfeld and fellow comedians go eat chicken and waffles together, and advertise cars on the side) and *Freunde von Freunden* (where arty careerist Europeans show off their carefully curated homes, offices, products, and dogs), to many other types of veiled bragging: terrorist training camp highlights; Christians trying to sell Rapture, and alt-right groups the 'Storm'; countless photographic compilations of thumbtacks, thimbles, antique weaponry, corkscrews, or Daily Carry; glitzy and glitchless performances of niche culinary tasks; tame discussions of periods and tampons; and giggly videos of boys trying on bras. The web is for lonely, needy, greedy show-offs and the people who love them.

Among those most suckered by the new technology of self-absorption are the most unhappy people on the planet: pre-pubescent and teenage girls. Young women rightly live in terror of the society in which they find themselves, understandably aspiring to reach adulthood *without* getting raped, shot, man-handled, murdered, trolled, or publicly discredited. It's ambitious of them. Huddling strategically behind their screens, *computer* screens, these girls have invented a new kind of purdah. From the safety of undisclosed locations (usually upper-middle-class American homes), they participate in their chosen amazeballs genre, a bottomless pit of boredom and twaddle: the cinematic low point known as the Morning Routine video.

These videos are short, quasi-home-made autobiographical films that record in a certain amount of intimate detail these girls' sheltered existences ('Just woke up!'). The final products are uploaded on to YouTube and elsewhere for the edification of an insular, supposedly all-girl audience (though anyone can tune in — anyone who can *bear* to, that is). The self-appointed and well-defended girl-stars welcome other (lesser) girls into their bedrooms (but only in the virtual sense), and in return get summarily liked or hated. (Let the bitching begin.) Each video thus functions as a daily workout for the barefaced, bug-eyed, belief-beggaring, bullshitting self — for both author and audience. If not exactly works of art, they are masterpieces of narcissism.

Product endorsement is the sinister inspiration behind much of what these girls inflict on one another. Alternately self-aggrandising and self-deprecating, affectedly awkward and sometimes flirty, these girls *seem* to want to be your pal, but it's the attention of multimillion-dollar cosmetics companies they really crave. Starbucks probably wins the Ubiquitous Product Placement award here though — hardly a single Morning Routine girl fails to demonstrate an allegiance to the incomprehensibly popular coffee brand. Even half-drunk pumpkin spice lattes from *yesterday* are worth tenderly recording on the bedside table, as proof of sophistication. Or the girl descends to the kitchen to concoct, barista-style, some sort of drink made out of Starbucks creams, syrups, and milk alternatives, from a stash of matching logoed canisters.

Another category of the Morning Routine video world is the Shopping Haul, rhyming conveniently with shopping mall. In these broadcasts, a dimpled teenybopper sits chummily on the floor of her bedroom, displaying bags of recently purchased clothing and her encyclopaedic knowledge of everything on offer (and Special Offer) at chain stores. She may emphasise that all this awesome stuff is like really really cheap, but is anyone fooled by this pose of frugality? Anyway, everything in this all-girl land is super-duper cute. Crazy-cute! And I mean *everything*. In a baking video, two cute girls make cute cupcakes out of cute ice-cream cones – all cute as can be. But how mercilessly would they diss any girl they knew who dreamed of eating one. Because anorexia's cute too.

MEN SHOULD BE FORCED TO WATCH THIS STUFF, TO SEE WHAT THEY'VE DONE TO WOMEN.

The slicker the whole shebang gets, the more effort the girls put into making things look humble. For atmosphere, the make-up tutorials feature deceptively amateurish product shots, with cutely shaky close-ups of every lip gloss, shampoo, perfume and itty-bitty container of wrinkle cream. Yes, wrinkle cream for twelve-year-olds.

To me, the make-up sessions seem *endless*, crazy-bad, with the juvenile mentor spending twenty minutes at a time basting her face like a Thanksgiving turkey. If you skip ahead ten minutes, she's still at it! Or she's straightening or curling her hair with an electric hot brush, a business that often seems to take about an *hour*, while the ditzy monologue goes on. These people are indefatigable, and clearly lead the most leisured lives on the planet. Ever been in such a rush you forgot to brush your hair or apply lipstick, deodorant, nail polish, jewellery? These girls never do, and by example they pressure other girls to spend hours and hours of *their* young lives too on this self-conscious prettifying. They even pretend it's fun, smiling non-stop while they administer the gunk. They seem to get a particular kick out of trying to hide their acne. It's all very upbeat, anyway.

Then there are the more serious sisterly advice talks, when they tell their viewers that friendship is a 'two-way thing', unhappiness a 'waste of time', water necessary, and that bees, yeah! 'bees make the world keep going'. In solipsistic Q & As, the funette answers 'questions' from viewers, such as what's your favourite item of make-up, or your OOTD (outfit of the day), or the craziest thing you ever did. In Mom Tags, another recurring strand of the genre, it's the *mother* who's quizzed on the craziest thing the girl ever did. There are also whole videos of hairdos, supposedly created in response to viewer demand. Hard to believe. Or, now and then, a ten-minute video on What's in My Purse. Here, the depressing contents of the poor chump's handbag (the contents of handbags are always depressing, because there's never enough MONEY in there) are dumped on the floor, so that she can mull over yeah! the mind-numbing purpose of each object. Why not dump out what's in the *bin* instead? Let's see the roaches, honey, the needles, the prophylactics... But drugs and sex have nothing to do with this particular web world. These are rich, pretty, artfully self-censoring princesses – *nuns* of a sort, showing off their habits.

The most unnerving thing about these videos is how *alone* the girl is. Despite the hazy form of a mom or sibling standing in the background sometimes, it seems highly likely the video girl was incubated and hatched in her bedroom by remote control, without human intervention. And there she continues her solitary reign. The bedroom is always surprisingly neat, the walls white or lilac, with the emphasis on the bed (always a double), her throne and pedestal. Lying there in stylish sleepwear, surrounded by scented candles and electronic devices, the girl studies herself on all available screens. The TV, laptop, smartphone, and mirror (or 'meer', as they all pronounce it) become interchangeable. The house beyond, occasionally glimpsed, is brand new, ostentatious, cleansed, and minimalist, with a comically well-stocked fridge. The girl appears to be in sole command of this empire, or wills herself to be. No sign at all of the retinue of servants either, who must actually keep the household afloat. Outside sits a BMW she claims is hers.

But what does she need a car for? Especially during a pandemic. Many of these self-chronicling shut-ins were already homeschooled *before* the lockdowns. They happily admit they hardly ever leave the house. 'I don't have anywhere crazy to go.' Their idea of an expedition is to sit on the *balcony*, where they complain that people in the outside world make noise, noise which interferes with the all-consuming video project and soon forces the girl to retreat indoors.

Little Kaspar Hausers, their only abiding interest is in looking, sounding, and, yeah! acting cool — so as to receive thumbs ups on their vlogs from people they will never meet. They are dolls come to life: they move their limbs, chatter, and change their clothes a lot. Their bodies are smooth, their skin blemish-free (almost). Other lonely, less cosmetically privileged girls are allowed to benefit from this shamanic performance. They can learn, for instance, how to carry on an endless soliloquy while applying the daily dolly mask that ensures they will prematurely age and require multitudinous ameliorating skin preparations for life. *Vita brevis, Noxzema longa.*

These girls have all mastered the Valley Girl accent and manner, even if their home valleys actually lie in Minnesota or Pennsylvania or, for all we know, Transylvania. It's always Christmas in July for them! Their conformism is totally standardised. But distress abounds, and not just in the denim cut-offs. Most of these young women are fearful and cranky, however serene their foreheads may be. They have been manipulated, they know it, and their revenge comes in handing on to fellow sad sacks an intimidating set of criteria for being acceptable. They're like all the girls you hated at school, and their airbrushed pretence of happiness is one of the most exasperating things about them. They rightly stare at themselves in the meer, wondering who's the unfairest of them all.

Why aren't these girls out saving whales, planting trees, building railroads, dismantling Guantanamo, dating people, or just reading a book? They do half-listen to *audiobooks* sometimes, books adapted for recent Hollywood offerings. But they're so 'crazy busy': they're pretend New Yorkers, hurriedly 'grabbing' a coffee, a bottle of water, their boots, and their car keys before they're 'good to go'. They live in envelopes of arid, pseudo-cosmopolitan nonchalance. They have fenced themselves off from our collective impending annihilation and, yeah! banished any hint of it from their speech, their looks, their demeanours and their boudoirs. Negativity has no place here (all the negative vloggers must have been burnt at the stake) and the prissiness is beyond belief.

The Morning Routine video issues from their YouTube *channel* (the hosts dwell on this word as if they believe they own whole TV networks) and sometimes begins with an intro, in which the kid flings her arms around a lot and wags her head alarmingly from side to side to make sure you know she's not just cute but full of irony. Then the 'routine' blasts off. The convention is that, as the filming begins, she's still asleep in bed – wearing a bra under her cutesome top, though, and crazy-comfy 'sweats' (sweatpants) perhaps. Her phone buzzes a wake-up call, she drowsily silences it, and then proceeds to spend a good amount of time lying in various angular poses on the bed, texting people and, yeah! checking social media. A memo of the mid-teen midriff. Sometimes a purse-dog or bunny rabbit joins her, to be cuddled (bunnies are big in this world, though the bunny itself must be small). Then, abruptly forgetting all about the squiffy pet, our hostess stumbles into her own private en suite bathroom.

No one excretes, of course, in this fairyland. Instead, at the sight of yet another meer, the girl starts dancing excitedly to her favourite music. And soon she's trotting, still in her PJs, through the echoing mansion to the fridge, which handily houses another video camera so that we can see her, yeah! exact facial expression as she decides what to eat. Her breakfast – yogurt, granola, fruit, and Starbucks – hints again at constipation. Then we're back upstairs to watch the exhausting make-up routine. It's, you know, I mean, yeah! it's like the worst sleepover you ever attended. Absolutely drained of mirth or interest. To liven things up a bit, she may take a shower, since she has at least four soapy liquid products to delightedly present. In the shower, Morning Routine girls wear *bikinis*: again, the whiff of the nunnery. Perhaps they fear some unfortunate sexual awakening might cause the collapse of this Eden in which everything's cute *except* boys.

Who watches this stuff? It's no great comfort that, for every Humbert Humbert who may be spying on Morning Routine videos to see budding adolescent girls acting kooky for the camera, there are probably dozens, if not hundreds, of faithful female contemporaries online, soaking up the atmos, thrilled to be spoken to nicely by *anyone*, even by a girl born to annoy.

Artificiality is a given, as is all the lying. It's like a cash-conscious *Clueless* – though these girls are backed by a certain level of wealth. Despite the pretence of artlessness and autonomy, most of the videos obviously get a lot of technical help. Since, the more energetic the camera angles, editing, lighting, and colours, the more hotel-like the domicile, and the more savage the dermabrasion, the happier the sponsors will be. Which is super-crazy-great.

You should see all the jars of brushes and eyebrow pencils, the array of eyeshadows and eyeshadow primers and eyeshadow concealers, the eyeliners and eyelash curlers and earlobe enhancers; the lipsticks, the lip exfoliators, the lip-slimers and lip-swellers; the cold cream, the foundation, the ointments, the unguents; the mists and sprays and monsoon mud packs; the scissors, the tweezers, the Dead Sea nail balm; the sponges and cotton balls and foam pads and pad foams and, yeah! all the hair-knuckle-undering machines! It's enough to satisfy an army of make-up artists on a Busby Berkeley picture. The shelving alone deserves an Oscar, with all the little totalitarian drawers of very well-organised stuff. With such pigments and such priorities, these kids should be painting the Sistine Chapel! Instead, Morning Routine art is ephemeral and all wiped away twelve hours later by the Night-time Routine.

There's a confessional element to these before-and-after cosmetic transformations: these girls are admitting to their fascinated viewers that channelling Barbie takes work. Even if yeah! you're like the prettiest girl in town already and just can't help it. To show that they're *human*, they often include a blooper reel at the end, and throughout the ordeal that is their lives, the girls are upbeat – because unhappiness is like such a waste of time. They lead eventless, nourishmentless, friendless, freedomless, and odourless lives – apart from all the fumes from the promotional sprays and scents and toners with which they hourly asphyxiate themselves. 'I get so many compliments on this perfume. Not that that's *why* we should ever do things. But it's *nice!*'

They are spatially-challenged cheerleaders, with blusher brushes for pom-poms, purse-pups as mascots, and the bedroom their field of dreams. Some of these home-based advertisers are under sixteen, incidentally, making them child labourers. Exploited by cosmetics firms, they in turn exploit their hoodwinked viewers, flaunting their sponsorships and luring the unwary toward their deranged music videos as well, which they also want to sell. Vulnerable to thumbs downs from across the globe on account of their asses (fat!) and eyebrows (thick!), their resolutely pally personas are perfect avatars of capitalism. The phenomenon isn't new. As Shirley Jackson put it in the fifties:

> From the time my daughter gets up in the morning to brush her hair the same number of times that Carole up the street is brushing *her* hair to the time she turns off her radio at night after listening to the same program that Cheryl three blocks away is listening to, her life is controlled, possessed, by a shifting set of laws... The side of the street she walks on, the

shoes she wears to walk on it, the socks, the skirt, the pocket-book… even the jacket and the haircut are rigidly prescribed.[1]

But those baby-boom popularity-seekers were spared the extra barbed wire of social media. Will our pampered twenty-first-century slave girls ever break free? Their YouTube, Instagram, Keek, and Vine experiments *could* turn into real girl power, yeah! if these ostriches could only find time for activism, between the waxing and waning of their daily beauty regimens. A little light political posturing might spark up those monologues too, and brighten the bleak days of their dotage – unless they just become online Miss Havishams, documenting their disintegration, with the Mourning Routine.

Come on, dump the face powder, gals. *This* is the stuff of girl dreams:

To turn somersaults naked, outdoors,
your cunt in the air.
To wallow in baths of whipped cream
and maraschino cherries.
To ride a galloping stallion bareback along a beach.
To understand the phases of the moon and Dog Star.
To be free as a mermaid adrift in the sea.
To run into a bullring and befriend the bull.
To discover something very very important.
To speak the language of goats and hoop snakes.
To be unique.
To fly.
To hide a pet mouse in your mouth and scare people.

---

1 *Let Me Tell You* (Penguin, 2015).

SING THE UNELECTRIC!

(In Praise of Buttons, Bikes, and Jam)

Once there was a world without power: without power stations, power surges, or power suits. A world in which, okay, people ruined their eyesight reading and sewing stuff in the dark. They also had the occasional accident on the stairs. Indoor plumbing still had a way to go too. But at least genes and gonads weren't permanently damaged by man-made radiation leaks, and light pollution from earth didn't keep the whole cosmos awake. They were spared so much, our ancestors: struggling with Teasmades and twin-tubs, microwaving cakes, and becoming self-taught computer technicians. They had it all – freedom, individuality, culture. They even had time to think. And then electricity was tapped, Henry Ford ruined civilisation with the private car, and Steve Jobs forced an Apple on us all.

A few years ago, I went to an exhibition at the Ashmolean Museum in Oxford of nineteenth-century Japanese silk embroidery. Probably not the best tapestries ever. They seem to represent an odd, slightly cheesy, cul-de-sac in the history of decorative arts, and are characterised by brightly coloured stitches crammed together against a black background of silk or velvet. They were mostly made for export, to please a taste for the oriental in England, America, and elsewhere. A lot of these tapestries are *frightful* pictorially, just idealised scenes in which excesses of silk and gold thread conjoin to produce lifeless souvenirs of hillside temples or tigers. One triptych screen of a life-size embroidered peacock offered the closest approximation of peacock feathers I've ever seen – but it was *not* a real peacock. It was a needless exercise in imitation.

Padded silk is an art form, it turns out, and an endearing one sometimes. One folding screen featured tiny labourers, village characters, and fancy ladies, all meticulously rendered in silk-padded bas-relief. Every detail of their garments was hyperreal, and the effect was stupendous. Maybe you have to sew a few thousand vulgar panels to come up with one good one. But even at their most grotesque, these silken offerings still had a dignity and verve that most printed images and photography lack. They exist, they *coexist* with us, they age, they breathe; they were very cleverly, painstakingly, put together by hand, *many* hands (mostly male hands, apparently), years ago. How much life had to be lived just to get the thing done! *Human time* was invested in these peculiar productions. And no electricity was involved.

The same goes for many denigrated handicrafts (usually the work of women): the elaborate and time-consuming culinary traditions of India, France, and Mexico, tapestry weaving, needlepoint, knitting, lace-making, basketry, batik, macramé, rug-braiding, knitting, crochet, gilding, quilting, or the long-lost art of dough pictures, whereby you stick thin layers of white dough on a dark background to make a bas-relief picture of Victorian milkmaids lugging water or making butter (maybe it was a way of using up leftover pastry). And all the other crafts with which people kept idle hands busy, like beadwork, coiled paper pictures, silhouette-cutting, stencilling, all those goofy foil and sequined pictures made from kits, soap sculpting, and gluing spray-painted macaroni on to the top of a cigar box.

Where are signs of the hand now? Within the alienating realm of digital technology and industrialisation, we're not just losing sight of what art is, but what the human hand can do. It's capable of a lot more than just texting, gliding a mouse around or separating Velcro. As James Joyce said about 'the hand that wrote *Ulysses*', 'It did lots of other things too.'[1] Hands are appendages of major importance! We wouldn't last a minute without them. Nobody would catch you when you're born, or affix you to the nipple, or change your nappy, or embrace and caress you. No matter how much we like machines, consumerism, and remaining motionlessness at the altar of Netflix, the human hand is our biggest love.

Not to see anything made by hand is a kind of death, a deprivation closely aligned to the prospect of never being touched again. Shaking each other's hand in greeting is an acknowledgement of the significance of hands. People have missed this during the era of Covid. Poking elbows at each other just isn't the same. Handbags are an extension of the hand. Thatcher was naked without her handbag.

〜

I'm tired of electricity, coal, gas, petrol, and especially nuclear power. I now only like the kind of energy that plants and animals

---

1 Richard Ellmann, *James Joyce* (Oxford University Press, 1959).

naturally expend going about their daily business. Electricity is a kind of ethereal rapist, interfering with everyone. It's a form of abuse. And I'm not talking electric shocks, just the devious way electricity insinuates itself into your house, into your life – and money drains out of the bank. We're not given any choice in the matter. We even read our electricity bills by electric light.

Not having electricity has long been a stigma, a sign of either poverty or incompetence. Most of us are convinced we *must have it* – as a result, hydroelectric companies throw people *out* of their homes in order to build more dams. It's amazing they get away with it. Electrification has taken the place of education, health, and financial benefits, as the one thing governments must provide – before developing countries get their mitts on it.

It's grown on me gradually, like a turtle shell, that I hate electricity. (Turtles are well-protected against electric eels.) It gives me a buzz to think about unelectric things. I get this warm, private, halogen-free glow. And I've begun almost unconsciously to search the world for anything that doesn't require electricity. I appreciate wrinkles in clothing now, because they imply an electric iron lying fallow somewhere. Dust bunnies under beds attest a dormant hoover. My attitude is not really a moral position, nor a hygienic or political one, though there are ample ways of defending it morally, hygienically, and politically. It's not merely melancholic either, derived from nostalgia and worry over the environment – though I do think my distaste originated the moment I learnt, as a child, that Lake Erie was officially dead, flooded with so many toxins from factories on its shore that no fish or plants could live in it any more. I wanted to get back to nature. This developed into a disdain for fashion, new buildings, the space programme, tree surgery, polyester, pharmaceutical companies, men with short hair, witch-burning, and the Industrial Revolution.

But I've recently observed in myself an acute disgust with all things pulsing, humming, and zapping, too, an awkward handicap in the modern world. I have an increased respect for simple stuff that doesn't move without help, stuff that just sits there, stuff that doesn't require the aid of power stations to animate or validate it. These artefacts may have *started* life in factories, through various uses of fossil fuel, but they've since rebelled against such parentage to claim a quieter, independent existence. Such noble and obliging things as keys, buttons (a *kind* of key: they open and shut your clothes for you), bidets, bathtubs, bicycles, butter, bells, belts, Band-Aids, balloons, blankets, books, beards, pens, paper, pisspots, pottery, poodles and parrots, shoes, sheds, sleds, skis, skates, wind-up clocks, musical instruments, hand tools, water taps, toilets, (non-electric) typewriters, (non-electric) toothbrushes (non-electric) tennis rackets, tulips in a glass of water, tables, chairs (who would want an *electric chair* – outside of Florida?), candles, matches, cupboards, clothing, Kleenex, corkscrews, cigarettes, needles and cotton thread, doorknobs, doors, hinges, drills, hammers, nails, screws, pliers, saws, see-saws, scales, sliding scales, corkscrews, home-made jams, and padded silk panels.

The wooden shutters in my bedroom, which keep out the light and the cold, were created before power tools, and can only be repositioned with human help. No external force, no artificial, doomed, or dwindling power source, is involved. And they work! They've lasted for two centuries. The duvet works too, without electricity, as do the drawers, shelves, floorboards, and rug. So, too, the pictures on the wall. My husband runs on his own steam too, especially when he's steamed about something.

We can even open and close our bedroom door without enlisting the services of the National Grid.

I admit there is also an old laptop in our bedroom. Such things jar. Plus, several environmentally unfriendly lamps – though not as many of them as a friend of mine would advise. She always says I have too few lamps, but I think she has too *many*. She lights up her home like an operating room, and would be wholly unsupportive of my aversion to electricity if I ever dared mention it to her.

I haven't yet reached so extreme a position on electricity that I have to retreat to the desert or up a tree. My electricity tolerance fluctuates. On a plane, I'm resigned to being saturated in electricity (including the risky proposition of flying through electrical storms). I more or less tolerate the little reading light and the fake fan overhead. The suck-you-uppo toilets, the blazing TV screens. The drinks trolley at least is hand-powered – such restraint! But, once at home again, I flee all these hateable things for stable, non-vibrating, non-blasting, non-grating, non-sapping, unexplosive and unelectric entities: fruit bowl, wine, plants, candlestick, husband, playing cards, baths, hot-water bottles, sellotape, pencils, scissors, paper, stone.

Why do we find computer screens so compelling? We can't stop looking at their glittering, glowing, jewel-like colours. They're the new stained glass. Perhaps we half-mistake them for *picture windows*, and feel an instinctive need to check them constantly for visitors, marauders, and weather changes. But computer screens *aren't* windows – they're prison bars! This subjection to a life of digital confinement is repeated by the billion, worldwide. You leave your office jail cell for your handy home prison, with your smartphone to shackle you like an electric tag on the journeys in between. And the 'cloud' now uses more electricity than *whole countries*.

Fantasies of electricitylessness: to live in a steading somewhere, equipped with a reliable well, vegetable patch, fireplace, wood-stoked Aga. Not a microwave or pressure cooker in sight. White wine chills in a gurgling spring just outside the door. Life would be all porridge and padded silk, a chicken or two pecking each other outside, and musical instruments, which we'd play to warm ourselves up. I would miss the ready supply of music recitals now provided instantly by YouTube or CDs. And washing clothes by hand would be a chore. Many household devices are addictive – cooker, kettle, fridge, freezer, toaster, dishwasher... But they take up so much space. It's time they all merged into one servile machine that would hoover things, dust things, toast and boil things, broadcast your favourite music non-stop, and cook up a stew too, through sheer friction while it's doing the housework. An iPlod.

But it would have to be silent. I can't stand the *noise* generated by these contraptions of ours. Industrial noises have driven people crazy since the beginning of mass production. Workers were deafened by nineteenth-century cotton mills. Now the noise has penetrated the domestic scene. I'd do anything not to have to hear an extractor fan ever again, or a washing machine on spin cycle, or *our shower*, which has begun to squeal at certain temperatures. Noise is a feature of our age. Why *manually* rake leaves, allowing your neighbours to sleep late, when you can frazzle everybody with a leaf blower? Why sweep the streets with brooms when you can send out an ineffectual little mechanical pavement sweeper with twirling brushes, suds squirters, and a cutesy name? In an alienating electronic voice, it wends its troubled way blindly down the street, leaving a little trail of water and dog shit wherever it goes. Sooty the Street Cleaner repetitively declares 'Attention. Take care. Pavement cleaning in progress' – from afar, it sounds like 'Buzz off buster, buzz off buster, buzz off buster...'

I recognise I'm fighting a losing battle – going up the down escalator – since everything is becoming more and *more* electric, not less. I am too! I watch too many movies and don't read enough books. And I used to write on an old typewriter. Typewriters, for your information, are twentieth-century machines that automatically printed what you wrote, without being asked, and never lost your work because you've forgot to 'save'. They didn't catch viruses, they didn't bother you with questions, questions, questions, and updates, and glitches, and reboots, and they cost almost nothing to run. Mine had very small type, which I particularly like. But here I am now, like everybody else, tapping out a Word document on a computer, staring at my individual light panel, with Pieter Wispelwey playing Bach's suites for solo cello to me on the same machine. Oh hell. I'm just another volt dolt. And most of my mail is email now. Physical letters, which were usually much better written than emails, are practically extinct. Posties risk Covid merely to deliver junk mail now.

What'll happen when every good, plain, manually operated mechanism is replaced with an electronic one? When your battery-powered lipstick whizzes uncontrollably across your face and your shoes lace themselves? (Too tight!) We're already being offered electric toilets, and electronic airline check-in and electronic key cards in hotels and universities. Maps have been outmoded by satnav, books by Kindle, Nook, Kobo and Audible, and the phone has been supplanted by Zoom, WhatsApp, Snapchat and Skype. Poker, solitaire, Scrabble, crossword puzzles, jigsaw puzzles, recipes, newspapers, shopping, and gambling have all been abducted into online existences.

You can't even have a baby any more without using vast amounts of electricity, though our ancestors somehow managed without, and most animals still do. We go from battery-operated sex toys to ultrasound scans to electric breast pumps and baby monitors. These are followed by baby computer games, baby TV shows, and baby food blenders. We wallow in dependence on electricity. As if there were never power cuts! Hospitals and factories all have to have back-up generators. After 2012's Hallowe'en hurricane, people in New York apartment buildings couldn't use the *elevators* or *toilets*. They had no water supply because city-wide power cuts meant the electric pumps were on the blink. It's no joke walking up fifteen flights with your dog and your groceries. The food in people's fridges and freezers rotted, and dialysis had to be rationed.

The more dependent we get on electricity, the more we're at the mercy of the energy providers. We have given up any illusions of self-sufficiency or manual dexterity to become electricity-purchasing units. Humans now exist only to establish more and more outlets for electricity and to make ever-increasing demands on it. Our entire culture is in hock to electricity. It doesn't serve us, we serve it. The pathos!

～

It would be wonderfully calm and quiet in our steading, and so *private*. No computers. When you're on a computer, a million advertisers, hackers, malware gremlins, and the FBI are always staring over your shoulder. Electronics are high-anxiety, high-maintenance novelties. The cost alone — everybody has to invest thousands of pounds in new IT equipment every few years, just to get their emails! (Computer enthusiasts *exult* in these equipment updates, like car fanatics obsessing over new car designs.) With all these machines clanking away for us, our increased immobility further disables us. We *try* to control our expanding bellies with walking machines and electric toning belts, and obliterate facial hair with electric shavers and electrolysis. Meanwhile, what little is left of the handmade or do-it-yourself continues to be obliterated in favour of the distant and virtual, a far less charitable commodity.

Bathed in artificial light, we're really back in the Dark Ages. No trace will be left of our culture soon besides climate change, millions of Nigella Lawson mixing bowls, the Gutenberg project (*maybe*), and the heaps of radioactive waste. I'd rather *walk* to London than take a train fuelled by nuclear energy. There's no feasible or responsible plan for dealing with nuclear waste and nuclear accidents. We have permanently ruined the environment in honour of electricity, in honour of Fukushima and Chernobyl. We're like kids with their new toys: we want stuff that requires electricity and we want it *now*. Entranced by the virtual, we've lost contact with the earth. We're impetuously, mesmerically, floating off into cyberspace. Insects will be pleased.

And the world was once so verdant! It was there to be loved. Despite the ravages of religion, war, tyranny, massacres, patriarchy and suspect Cornish pasties, there was at least some guilt-free joy in the natural world. Look at Tobias Smollett, writing about Glasgow.[2] Think of it, *Glasgow*.

2　*The Expedition of Humphry Clinker* (1771).

Glasgow... is one of the prettiest towns in Europe... From Glasgow we travelled along the Clyde, which is a delightful stream... Here is no want of groves, and meadows, and cornfields...

Groves? Streams? But things were still beautiful then, just a few hundred years ago – before the industrialists backed us all away from nature with our hands held over our heads. 'Nothing to see here.' I know there was no whooping cough vaccine. But there was a whopping amount of clarity, not just in the air and the water but in people's *minds*. Now we go to war over unsustainable forms of energy. Our romance with fossil fuels has peaked in absurdity.

Skateboards are electrified now, but skis are still human-powered. Rafts require nothing but a handheld paddle. Or you can just sit on one and let the current take you where it will. Sailboats only need a sail (and a good sailor). And there's always the bicycle, the pedalled kind. Suspended on your little seat, with the wind in your hair (or helmet). A bike proceeds at a human pace (usually), and you can park one anywhere, unlike a car, which is just a two-tonne metal box and killing machine, ravenous and needy. Maybe we should use up all the remaining electricity to manufacture *bikes*, and then just *turn it off*.

Know what works fine without electricity? Night-time. We all endure a nightly electricity fast without harm (unless you're dependent on an electric blanket, electric alarm clock, a night light, or an iron lung). You can sleep right through these low-tech periods of darkness, or get up and enjoy the quiet.

Another unelectric thing is people. And animals. They're not electric *yet*, anyway – make the most of them now, before they're all replaced with robots.

This world is too expensive, too ugly, too heartless, too hand-less to bear! Where's art, where's kindness and comfort? Where are the simple, amiable, graspable products of our labour? All I'm saying is that when the primordial shit hits the electric fan and all current sources of energy are gone, *I* will have books, pencils, paper, index cards, a hole puncher, candles, matches, needles and thread, soap, socks, sweaters, long johns, a working loo (I *hope*), quite an assortment of ink stamps, some paintings I really like, old photos, a plain old manual toothbrush, a type-writer, and a wind-up torch. What'll you have?

AH, MEN

Every now and then people bafflingly try to depict the late Doris Day as some sort of feminist trailblazer or iconoclast. Doris Day was one of the corniest cream cakes ever produced by male self-love: not just the goofy girl next door but the goody-goody *bore* next door who put up with anything her nutso 1950s neighbours, and Rock Hudson, asked of her. By playing frisky nitwits, she was seamlessly sucked into the misogynistic vortex at the centre of our punitive culture. Like Monroe, Garland, Goldilocks, Medea, Medusa, Salome, Lady Macbeth, and Shirley Temple, Doris Day materialised from deep in the collective male psyche to become just another gal to kick around. It's depressing.

'Ah, men,' as Bette Davis would say.[1] I'm sorry to have to mention this, but men don't like women much. They subtly let us know this from time to time, through rape, murder, public stonings, porn, prostitution, female circumcision, anti-abortion laws, the pay gap, constant scoldings (online and in person), and sulking when you win at Scrabble. Though forever in the wrong,

---

1 *All About Eve* (directed by Joseph L. Mankiewicz, 1950).

men are not gracious in defeat. Hence the geyser of fury they exude. Ciudad Juárez in Mexico is now famed for its femicide rate. Congrats. As a beleaguered Honduran woman recently told the *New York Times*, 'Just because you are a woman you feel hatred. Like someone is always trying to kill you.'[2]

Why do men let us live at all? It must really go against the grain to see us still trotting about, after all their efforts to defeat us. Are they just *humouring* us while they farm us for our vaginas?

Of course there are men I love, men I admire, I admit it, and a fair number I put up with. Hell, I put up with them all! We *all* do. But that doesn't mean they're good for humanity. It's *women* we need in charge of things: they're much less emotional, and far more likely to have their priorities right, such as life, liberty, and the pursuit of happiness. Also, as Fran Lebowitz has said, they rarely rape their employees.[3]

Women have a lot of latent power. Think of all the stuff we do – paint, teach, write, sing, dance, compose, medicate, self-medicate, vote, quit, quilt, invent, invest, divest, divorce, ponder, squander, and produce young. We go to the gym, to the moon, to the dogs, to the morgue. It's a multitasking nightmare! We even dare call ourselves 'Dr' if we happen to have a PhD, despite being belittled for it – in Jill Biden's case, by an irritated male columnist in the *Wall Street Journal* who patronisingly redubbed the new First Lady 'kiddo'.[4]

UXORIOUSNESS SHOULD HAVE BEEN THEIR BUSINESS.

Instead, men still use marriage as a stick to beat us with. A

---

2 'Someone Is Always Trying to Kill You' (*New York Times*, April 5, 2019).
3 'Who's Afraid of Fran Lebowitz?', All About Women Festival, March 6, 2018 (Sydney Opera House Talks and Ideas Archive).
4 Joseph Epstein, 'Is There a Doctor in the White House?...' (*Wall Street Journal*, December 11 2020).

woman's marketable charms have merely broadened to include her financial assets as well as her ass. Doris Day did her best sixty years ago to help forge the path of obedience, in her usual role as the single career girl in search of a husband to complete her (after mildly competing with her). In a male world, women juggle home life and working life. Men just go to work.

Women are also made to seem responsible for everything that happens in a marriage. People are always blaming wives for fattening their husbands up, for instance. But what if it's the other way around? What if it's *men* who make *women* fat, with their customary insistence on three meals a day? Some women are frightened off living with men because of all the eating involved. They write to agony columns about it! There are all those 'hangry' grumps too, on the 5:2 diet, who make Mondays unbearable for everyone in their vicinity. People don't talk enough about the metabolic strains on marriages.[5] Men make you cold, get you fat, then ditch you for somebody warmer and thinner, and act all innocent about it.

༄

Amazingly, men are still deciding if we'll *do*, in the flame-choked, tsunami-soddened, silicon-breasted, carcinogen-ripened world they created for us, this great big radioactive cowpat of Growth and Progress and Pointlessness they've deposited everywhere.

Body-shaming is on the increase. Thanks to the ubiquity of porn, young women are now expected to produce a whole new

---

5 Differences of opinion on the ideal temperature of the home is another example of metabolic discord. Men often object to the thermostat being turned up, and prefer to see female life partners shiver.

level of nubility. It's not just putting a 'face' on that has reached a horrific level of professionalism. There's now the designer vagina. A global effort is underway to stamp *out* female genital mutilation, yet women in the West lust after elective labial surgery. Can you *get* any more dutiful than believing all vulvas have to be the same, even if achieving this uniformity involves excruciating pain? You can't even SEE the damn thing (the entire trade in pared-down pudenda is reliant on the male gaze). Add to this the customary scored-out pubic triangle: reduced by shaving and waxing to a narrow landing strip, the trimmed vulva is today's must-have signal of subservience. Is it for fear men will *miss* the vagina completely and head off with their joysticks into the stratosphere?

In guilty mimicry of female hair removal, *men* have started shaving themselves from top to bottom too! Everyone has to be hairless, just in case they're called upon to perform in a porn movie at any moment. You have to be expert in sex toys too, the Kama Sutra, S & M, bondage, striptease and pole-dancing. Sexuality is now Olympian in its competitiveness.

The obsession with bodily eligibility is a great distraction (along with *The Crown*, *Bridgerton*, the *actual* Olympics, and other forms of bread and circuses), from the real calamities of our times: racism, sexism, and climate change. Instead of confronting men about all these lousy ideas of theirs, women engage in a lifelong beauty competition, expensively daubing the face and fighting the flab while men distinguish themselves through acts of aggression and beefing about what's in the fridge.

Yet it's women who apologise and apologise! Our whole posture, our whole mode of being, is apologetic – when we have nothing to apologise *for*. Women's crimes come nowhere near what men have done. Who invented genocide, totalitarianism, whaling, rugby, and snuff movies? Or those medieval skimming-ton parades in which women deemed argumentative 'shrews' were dragged through the village, followed by a ducking? Who invented the goddam atomic bomb?

MEN HAVE RUINED LIFE ON EARTH.

How do patches of cellulite, unthreaded eyebrows, the occasional burnt pound cake, sharp word, or crying jag compare to *that*? After *men* get through with us all, only a few viruses will survive – viruses, prions, buckyballs and carrier bags.

Men delight in unauthorised violence, but glory in *legalised* murder too, protecting pugnacity with an official stamp. How eagerly they cosy up to armies, warfare, war movies, military history, or any kind of uniform – they love to be drenched in camo or battleship grey. Give them a big grim death-promoting system they can glom onto, a male hierarchy that provides them with goals, loyalty, doom, destruction, epaulettes, good opportunities for rape, a general miasma of testosterone, a guaranteed pass on domesticity, and a stage for showy acts of heroism, and they're happy as clams. They can't even write about *beer* without bringing war into it:

> Thanks for choosing to spend the next few minutes with this special homicidally hoppy ale. Savour the moment as the raging hop character engages the Imperial Qualities of the Malt Foundation in mortal combat on the battlefield of your palate![6]

Talk about killing yourself with drink. It almost makes you mourn the lost art of duelling. One good thing about duels was

---

6 From a bottle of Lagunitas IPA.

that a single confrontation could potentially rid the world of two idiots.

༈

The other thing men like is *crime*. Crime's had a good long innings during patriarchy. We've had crooks, hoodlums, knaves, rogues, renegades, seducers, agents provocateurs, insurrectionists, pirates, scamps, scoundrels, scaramouches, scallywags scapegraces, quacksalvers, mountebanks, rapscallions, charlatans, backsliders, black sheep, and bad eggs. We've bred fraudsters, felons, forgers, royal families, chisellers, cheaters, con artists, traitors, impostors, wage thieves, identity thieves, bike thieves, horse thieves, dog thieves, cat burglars. Grave robbers, pickpockets, shoplifters, slum landlords, shoddy builders, parole violators, bail jumpers, human traffickers, racketeers, snitches, squealers, superspreaders, and card sharks. Our lives have been blighted by hedge fund managers, embezzlers, pyramid and Ponzi schemers, perfidious perjurers, scammers, slanderers, libellers, stock brokers, insurance brokers, money launderers, insider traders, offshore bankers, lobbyists, monopolists, tax evaders, bribe takers, poisoners, and plagiarists. Libertines, adulterers, liars, fakers, fakirs, truants, malingerers, gold-diggers, lounge lizards, practical jokers, time and motion men, industrial spies and saboteurs, wastrels, vandals, smugglers. Flashers, stalkers, drink spikers, stickup men, kidnappers, pornographers, assassins, unelected despots, whisky waterers, collection box nickers, washing-line marauders, and photo-doctorers. Hijackers, human rights abusers, Holocaust deniers, drunk drivers, bootleggers, lynch mobs, public enemies, manslaughterers, cut-throats, hit-and-runners, chainsaw massacrers, bombers, spree-shooters, polluters, the criminally negligent, ricin mailers, shite hairdressers, Nazis, Tories, Republicans, Brexiteers, and book borrowers.

We obviously get some kind of kick out of transgression. Our mythology, folklore, balladry, historical records, and the annals of aristocracy rely almost entirely on the noteworthy actions of chancers, barbarians, and piss-takers. Sin and guilt, strange satellites of crime, have provided lucrative territory for religions too. There are elephants who storm villages, and macaques who seize people's smartphones to use as ransom at the Uluwatu temple in Bali.[7] But, of all animals, humans seem to make the best criminals. Do kangaroos court mayhem, plot insurrection, seethe with egotism, vanity, and resentment, and exult in deception and vengeance? Rarely. But with humans, as Trump and his cronies have proven, one traitorous tax-avoiding genocidal dumb-as-shit jerkball at the helm is never enough. It seems we want whole stacks of them.

Only in such a brutalised society could a sci-fi horror action drama like *The Terminator* become enshrined as family fare.[8] Right at the beginning, Arnold Schwarzenegger tears somebody's heart out with his bare hands – on camera – and then goes on to shoot a gun-seller and an innocent woman in the face, at close range. (Why is it always the *face*?) The woman is executed merely because she shares the same name as the Terminator's intended victim. I forget why the gun-seller's obliterated. That's as far as I got – there's only so much nonsense a person can stand – but I gather it's a bloodbath: the IMDb estimates the

---

7 'Study finds macaques go for tourists' electronics and wallets over empty bags and then maximise their profit' (*Guardian*, January 14, 2021).
8 Directed by James Cameron (1984).

death count at thirty-nine and, perhaps in deference to our love affair with crime, most of them are cops. I think the police should be *defunded*, but that's taking it too far.

Or how about the seemingly civilised movie *American Beauty*? What appears at first to be a gentle domestic satire ends inevitably in a shooting. Well, this is America, after all. What you get here is not so much suburbia personified as suburbia puréed. As if the only way to shut all these caricatures up – the homophobic ex-army dad, the bummed-out teenagers, the acquisitive and secretly lascivious mom, the underappreciated onanistic husband – is to shuffle them all into a crime scene. What if *It's a Wonderful Life* ended with someone shooting Jimmy Stewart in the head? Movies used to have a little tact. Now, the answer to all plot points is to blow somebody's brains out. It's Hollywood's *raison d'être*: bullet envy.

And then there's crime *writing*. Writing genre fiction of any kind is a cop-out. (Would it *kill* those people to write something fresh and new? Something honest and original? Something beautiful even?) But, of all the genres, from horror, sci-fi, cli-fi, po-mo, and chick lit, to travel, sex-and-shopping, speculative, supernatural, fantasy, historical, adventure, thrillers, war stuff, spy stuff, mob stuff, monsters, UFOs, etc., etc., nothing sinks lower in celebration of human lousiness than crime fiction. And it's usually such bad writing too! So lazy, so hackneyed, so awkward and mechanical – it *has* to be, to convey the stupid story and attendant clues. There's little room for organic flow. The plots are prone to sagging. Yet I once got into trouble merely for suggesting crime novels are 'overrated'. I didn't say they shouldn't exist, I didn't say nobody should read them, I didn't say their authors should be arrested for crimes against humanity – though it's tempting. All I said was, in response to a question about which book I felt was overrated: 'All crime fiction, I don't care who it's by.'[9] The backlash was startling. In tones familiar to anyone who reads Twitter or delves into the Comments section beneath online articles (never go below the line!), one disappointed *Guardian* reader called me ignorant, another said I was an asshole, and one wrote me right off: 'I was done with Lucy Ellmann when she was shitty about crime novels.'

Crime writers took it especially bad, and those people are *scary*. They know how to murder you every which way from Sunday! But I wasn't trying to burn their crummy books: censorship is even worse than the vice of writing godawful fiction. I just get tired of hearing crime fiction writers and crime fiction readers contend that these nasty ghastly novels are not only genuinely literary (they're not) but also some kind of validation of right over wrong, or a vital way of pinpointing and rooting out our darker tendencies. As if they're trying to *help* us in some way, striving to warn and educate us! I don't buy it. Nothing is being identified or conquered here. Nothing's being solved either. Nothing generous is being offered. All that's happening is that a lot of characters' eyeballs are being plucked out (and very remuneratively so for the writers). We are back in Ancient Rome: a murder mystery allows us the schadenfreudian fun of watching other people get mutilated. And in the case of crime fiction, that's usually women. Some readers evidently require such gruesome fairy tales nightly, so as to go on living in an unsafe, male-oriented world. Maybe solving one isolated mystery is simpler than facing how messed-up the whole bloody system is. Death struggles and near-death throes may even

---

9 'Books that made me', *Guardian* (August 16, 2019).

give ghoulish types a pleasurable adrenaline rush. Or, more legitimately, they may act as memento mori, an impetus to wise up. Or perhaps they spur in some the will to live. They quell mine. So, read your penny dreadfuls if you must, but have the taste not to mention it.

Accused of inexpertise on the subject, I proudly accept the slur. But I've read enough of the genre to form an opinion. Chandler rises above the rest – he's worth it for the wordplay. Highsmith's no stylist, she's repetitive and tedious and dreary. *But* she's rightly more interested in psychology than crime, which somehow makes her books ideal for an arduous plane trip. Agatha Christie's atrocious, only suitable for people with colds. And old Sherlock Holmes is barely a notch above Poirot and Miss Marple. What hacks these writers are.

On first reading it long ago, I did enjoy *The Moving Toyshop* by Edmund Crispin for some long-forgotten reason.[10] I think I approved of the way it scooted quickly past the crime to get on with the sleuthing. Looking at it again now, I find I've totally forgotten everything about it (another telling feature of most crime writing), including the runaway carousel scene at the end that Hitchcock stole for *Strangers on a Train*.[11] Here's what irks me about crime novelists: they can't even be bothered to think up something plausible, despite the ready supply of *actual* crimes in the world to study. And they're so reliant on coincidence, it's embarrassing. Is it likely that a man, off on a spur-of-the-moment trip from London to Oxford, would remember to bring a torch and a gun? A poet yet, named Cadogan. Did everyone own a gun in 1946? Maybe. Things were still unsettled

---

10 Gollancz (1946).
11 1951.

after the war perhaps. But still, make an effort, Crispin. Keep it real.

The murder plot is elaborately and shamelessly fanciful. Cadogan himself described it as 'strictly meaningless'! Crispin's memory of the layout of Oxford, though often pertinent to the story, often seems askew. And the baddies keep repetitively knocking people out with some sort of death grip on the neck – a technique I don't think it's very wise to spread around. (NB. I could never be a detective. Crispin's Gervase Fen is always springing up to use the phone! He's the most willing telephoner you ever saw. It would take me *weeks* to make even *one* of those phone calls, and by then the case would've gone cold.[12])

Mild times. Current fads in crime writing and Nordic noir seem to be all about gritty forensic enquiries into human horridness. Okay, enquire away. But don't pretend it's art, jewel-like in its finesse or complexity; nor that you're performing some kind of public service. Crime writers are in it for the money and their only job is to envelop a corrupted public in more and more examples of human depravity. Why would anyone research and write this guff *except* for money? So, sell out if you must, but there's no call for pride here. Gerald Ratner had the guts to admit his jewellery was crap.

What people don't object to enough about crime fiction is its maintenance of the misogynistic status quo. Just as war

---

12 In the book's favour, Crispin's asides can be nicely humorous, and I like the way his characters fall into literary chit-chat in the midst of trouble: the friendly lorry driver is a Lawrence fan, the Chief Constable has a *Measure for Measure* obsession. (Which suggests most people would prefer to think about something else, *anything* other than crime.) But Crispin's snotty about the murder victim's 'spinsterhood', a character flaw deduced on Cadogan's first sight of the corpse (with the aid of that handy torch): 'the flatness of her breasts suggested that she was unmarried.' Wow. So, there's the real crime: being flat-chested and single. Get a hold of yourself, man.

movies, even anti-war movies, inescapably glorify war, crime fiction romanticises the hell out of crime, no matter how many female detectives you proffer, nor how many sexist outrages they manage to sort out. You're still reinforcing an interest in patriarchal behaviour patterns that damage women. Our fixation on fictional criminality might seem innocent enough if there weren't such an obvious parallel between the invented visions, on paper, of women being sliced up and silenced, and the concurrent enactments in real life.

Quite clearly a lot of men still feel they have a right to decide if women live or die, fictionally or not. For some time now, Karen Ingala Smith has been compiling the Counting Dead Women project, a list of women murdered by men in the UK (there were about a hundred in 2020). But I agree with my friend Eloise Millar[13] that Ingala Smith should start *another* list: Counting Fictional Murdered Women. There must be MILLIONS by now, and almost as many murder methods, along with all their associated cults and copycat killers like the much-beloved Black Dahlia mystery, the Manson family, Jack the Ripper and all the rest of them, these tragedies multiplied beyond trace for our entertainment.

Refusing to read crime novels is a feminist act. But what about all those *female* crime writers, you cry, and their hordes of bloodthirsty female fans who turn up in droves at crime fiction festivals, avid for the next serial psycho dismemberer to hit the shelves? This is simply one of patriarchy's many perverse effects on the female mind. Women have been subjected to several thousand years of disenfranchisement and abuse. So, like any other colonised population, they're full of self-hatred.

---

13 Co-founder of the great Galley Beggar Press.

They have now picked up a habit of punishing themselves with lashings of imaginary violence – just as we routinely frighten our children with horrific bedtime stories.

Women may also read crime fiction for practical tips on self-defence: feeling vulnerable and demoralised, and well aware of male animosity towards them, female crime addicts prepare themselves for disaster by studying the territory and the criminal mindset, while also rehearsing fight or flight moves. Their brutish predilection for gore suggests the need for therapeutic repair work, not censure. Give women a peaceful, nurturing environment, give them a little self-respect and a sense of safety, give them *hope* that they are not in imminent danger of being garroted, trapped in a dungeon, or dissected at any moment, and they may no longer fixate on these terrifying tales of death and woe.

But why do MEN read this stuff? And write it? What do *they* get out of crime fiction except the chance to gloat over their own petrified paternalism and misanthropy? They cherish it like their prosthetic sex arse equipment. They want it because it does them no good at all, but it does violate women. The truth is, men don't need to know more about crime, they need to know *less*, they need to *unlearn* what they already know, the mess they invented. They need re-education and rehabilitation. They need a firm hand. They need to *discard* maledom, not burst their brains expanding on it and profiting off it.

How about working on the unsolved crimes of *environmental devastation* instead, or the chicanery of depriving people of healthcare, the petty larceny of monarchs, or the hoax of trying to resurrect Doris Day every decade or so?

TAKE THE
MONEY, HONEY[1]

The simplest proof that patriarchy's based on a load of lies,
all lies – and that men are stinkers – is the way servants were
treated just a century ago. In Britain, while the upper classes
swanned about pretending, nauseatingly, that women were frail,
helpless vessels incapable of serious thought or deed (there'd
have been a lot less swooning if they'd just loosened up those
corsets), the skivvies, 'slaveys', or aptly named 'maids of all
work', toiled sixteen hours a day with hardly an afternoon off,
emptying slops and lugging pails of water up and down flights
of stairs, tending a million hearth fires, washing floors, and
cooking, shopping, and ironing, all while being reprimanded,
slandered, harried, underfed, and routinely molested by their
'masters'. If rebellious, they were quickly torpedoed from the
household: those impossible people, the well-respected writers

---

1 As Audre Lorde said, 'The power you waste is being used against us' (https://
youtu.be/OUXjoBVQkpw).

Thomas and Jane Carlyle, kicked one of their maids out for giving birth (very quietly too) in a china closet. Such abuse was essentially a legal form of slavery: servants were kept in unhealthy conditions and paid a pittance (or *less*, due to breakages and other supposed deficiencies), while they ministered to the status quo.

Despite men's much-applauded upper-body strength, somehow it's *women* who are still the main skivvies today, performing as maids of all works, or sometimes as presidential press secretaries. Behind every man who helps with the housework, there's a tired woman following him around *thanking* him for helping with the housework. Male domination hasn't gone away, it's simply hidden itself behind a pretence of equality and a rather too convenient blurring of the gender divide. This game is still in play and thrives, like Trump and his buddies, on the power of IDIOCY.

A guy in England beat up his wife on their wedding night. But he had a reason: she'd asked him to help her take off her wedding dress.[2] I guess foreplay's a thing of the past. Imagine if she'd asked him to take out the trash!

Look, haven't we all had just about enough of men's idea of a good time? Drones, beheadings, *The Bullingdon Club*? Factory farming? Polluting every available body of water – and then *charging* you for a bottle of drinking water! Soon they'll be charging us for AIR too, the air they've filled with petrol fumes, stone dust, cow burps, asbestos, and nanoparticles, as well as smoke from all their stupid factories, stupid cigars and stupid barbecues.

---

2 'Bride beaten by new husband... because he couldn't get her dress off' (*Daily Mirror*, February 16, 2015).

Them and their goddam Industrial Revolution – which, when I was at school, was spoken of with such reverence! Agriculture and tree-clearance started to upset ecology long ago, but heavy industry has ruined the ozone layer, so that now we have record droughts and floods and hurricanes and blizzards in places that used to be habitable, and walruses have nowhere to lay their heavy heads. All to enable a few bellicose bully boys to make a mint. 'Make a buck, make a buck. Even in Brooklyn it's the same,' as Alfred says in *Miracle on 34th Street*.[3]

The pesticides, the herbicides, the murder–suicides! Institutional racism and sexism. Freemasonry. Online backgammon. School shootings. Diablo chicken wings. Breweries, microbreweries, whoppers and sliders, nanobytes and gigabytes and terabytes – men like anything that's either really big or really small. I wonder why.

And all the penile neckties. They never tire of them. Men are so *repetitive*! Them and their neon trainers and football scarves and football shirts and football hooliganism and baseball caps and baseball games and baseball mitts and baseball cards and other baseball memorabilia. Their dissertations on Spider-Man comics. Their lust for every sort of nonsense, for exclusive clubs and secret handshakes, for embezzlement and tax breaks and presidential pardons and golden showers and the unpardonable electric chair...

These pursuits come in tandem with their wilful, ruinous indifference to the enormities they have perpetrated on women's lives: through domination, violation, and the objectification of women's bodies, including their scorn for menstruation, gestation, parturition, and lactation, all that yucky female stuff

---

3 Directed by George Seaton (1947).

that is, incidentally, essential to mammalian survival (which Spider-Man isn't). What would become of us all if *men* had to breastfeed? When there's so much pinball to be played and gun barrels to be oiled, so many noteworthy trains coming and going and pints of beer waiting to be drunk? Babies would starve.

The sausages, so many SAUSAGES! Along with sausage-shaped pens, bullet trains, guns, missiles, space rockets, sky-scrapers, columns, plinths, obelisks, and towers. They have littered the globe with phallic symbols and equestrian statues, hedge funds, gold futures, sub-prime mortgages, and obstruc-tions of justice. Also, Mafia rings, cement feet, arms deals, urban blight, suburban sprawl, crack cocaine, misleading election fraud allegations, and those horrible khaki-coloured fisher-man's vests they wear, the ones with all the pockets. Not to mention all their damn *fetishes*: for steak, coins, stamps, guns, fishing tackle, cricket, racing, Moleskine notebooks, tool-kits, gadgetry, potato chips, birds, butterflies, Nasa, the soiled undies of schoolgirls, antiquarian memorabilia, exclusive brands of shaving cream, electronics, more electronics, high heels, rubber gear, leather gear, cars, motorbikes, unbelievably expensive hi-fi set-ups, apps, abs, six-packs, tobacco, boastful fables of derring-do, quantum theory, golf, lad mags, Mahler, Wagner, and Bob Dylan (they never shut up about *him*).

We're dying over here, man! We're snoring in the aisles and you don't even notice. I'm particularly tired of having to listen to them all play the guitar.

Them and their capitalism and their corporations and con-niptions and philosophical convictions, their nihilism, their defeatism, their elitism, their egotism, their optimism – inex-plicably conjoined with their love of apocalypse – and all the other huge fatal male cop-outs, all the *crummy ideas* we've had to stomach for the last five thousand years, while men barely even acknowledged that women EXIST.

They have proven themselves *apocalyptically* unfit to govern. Women would do a better job with their hands tied behind their backs (which, of course, they often are).

Why *do* women work for men? Not only that, but now we twerk for them too! Look at us, traipsing abjectly around our polluted earth, planning the supper! Always trying so hard to be *nice*. Having to *beg* for a few measly reproductive rights, a break in the wife-beatings, or just a little help with the dishes. Poking our pink parasols up at glass ceilings, tap, tap, tap... It's so demeaning – especially when you're twerking at the same time.

Women now bring home the bacon and *cook* it too. And men praise us for our *autonomy* – which leaves them free to watch their requisite ten hours of porn a day, decide on gender quotas, and pollute rivers.

But why *should* women work, why should we pay for *any-thing*, when we've been robbed blind for centuries? And I do mean blind. And yet there are women in this world who refuse alimony, preferring a 'clean' break. An attempt at resentment mitigation? Please. This is no way to behave!

Let's just forget equality, okay? It's dopey, it's insane! EQUALITY DOESN'T WORK.

It's a half-measure. This is an emergency – we've got to think big. To end sexism, racism, violence against women, worldwide bombing campaigns, and avert the coming ecological catastrophe, women need to get their hands on the reins, and fast. In fact, forget the reins, just grab the cash.

Sadly, in the current mercenary scheme of things, power rests on wealth and property, and is therefore mostly in male hands. Land ownership is an offensive idea but, if the world must be owned by anyone, let it be women.[4] Once in charge of things, women can institute a system of *common* ownership, with everything shared amongst women and animals. (Men can have a beer allowance.)

Men need to pay us what we're owed. Not just money. We're owed orgasms, we're owed world peace. I know, I know, I sound like Miss America when I start talking about peace. Hey, they owe us for *that* too, all those beauty contests we've had to sit through! And John Wayne movies. Men owe us for all the lip-smacking, wolf-whistling, catcalling, ass-pinching, crone-bashing, gun-slinging, cotton-picking gas-guzzling that's ever gone on.

And as for orgasms, the problem with men is, they think sex is for *them*. Let's get this straight once and for all:

SEX IS FOR WOMEN.

Throughout nature, it's *female* pleasure that counts, reproductively speaking. The female multiple orgasm tops any humdrum climax a penis can achieve. Sorry, guys, that's just the way it is. Life isn't always fair.

Men got everything about sex topsy-turvy. They invented monogamy and homophobia because they suffer so terribly from jealousy. But it's *men* who should be monogamous; women should be freewheeling. It's a shame to waste all that orgasmic capacity.

Men should pay us back for their belittlement of women. (It would take an eternity.) *Pay* us for their vulgarising of sex; for prostitution; for the invention of the phone, the camera, the gun, the car, the airplane, the internet, TV, nuclear power, liposuction, and tanning salons. *Pay* for the puny percentage

---

4 'If you put money in the hands of women, they can do magic.' UN women's representative Comfort Lamptey, speaking about Margaret C. Snyder's life's work (*New York Times* obituary, February 5, 2021).

of rape convictions. *Pay* for the cyclones and forest fires, *pay* for the poisoned water. *Pay* for the world wars, *pay* for toxic waste. *Pay* for atom bombs and chlorine gas and all the Nobels they awarded themselves for creating them. *Pay* for the gas chambers while they're at it, and animal extinctions, child soldier indoctrination, and the desecration of ecosystems. *Pay* for Hitler, Mao, Columbus, King Tut, Genghis Khan, Trump, Giuliani, the Proud Boys, and the Ku Klux Klan. Why not, why shouldn't they pay and *pay*?

They can pay for the pay gap too.

Once women control all the money, we can start reversing the fatal destructiveness of men. During this transition period, by the way, we won't need any male carping. Men are always so *critical*, jeez. A three-year ban on the male voice in public would be a big help: women will need time to think about how to *fix* this mess.

Any man in possession of a moral conscience should instantly recognise the logic and justice of these ameliorative measures and start forking out. NOW.

But it's not enough for well-meaning men to offer women their money. Women have got to *take* the money, and without shame. Why even show gratitude? *It's our bloody money.* We and our female ancestors earned it – the hard way.

So take the money, honey. And let's have no neg-head downer shit about being a kept woman or something. That sort of consideration is a luxury of the past. This is no time for self-doubt, self-abnegation or charity. No time to go Dutch on dinner either, or share the mortgage repayments. The world's going to hell in a handbasket, and something's got to be done about it! (Somebody do something about that 'handbasket' expression too.) The time has come for all good women to peacefully plunder. Yanking cash out of male hands is a humanitarian act. It's your new job, it's your right... and it's our only hope.

TAKE THE MONEY HONEY.

Don't sing for your supper, sing for *yourself*, as Bizet's Carmen would say – okay, bad example, since Carmen gets killed by her idiotically jealous boyfriend. Ah, men. They love to have the last word, even in operas. Listen to Helen Humes instead, with her astute 'Million Dollar Secret'.[5] (In essence? Find a rich man and make sure his will's made out to you.)

We will of course have to battle against some pretty powerful mind games. We've been bullied for centuries into believing there's something terrible about being branded a whore, slut, floozy, or gold-digger. What a clever male trick *that* was, when whores had it right all along! Not in terms of contorting your sexuality or risking your life to please men, no, but in terms of TAKING THE MONEY.

Why are we still trying to figure this out? *Men* can't handle money! Look what they do with it: Harley-Davidsons, Doc Martens, vintage steam train rides, the stock market, Lolita islands, big-game hunting, and the cultivation of giant vegetables. Men are *crazy*. They're always calling *us* crazy, but men are completely off the beam. They must have lost the plot some time ago. You can tell by all the tornado-chasing.

Now, there may be a tricky interval there, during the female-oriented redistribution of wealth, when newly enriched and empowered women will be bombarded by lounge lizards, murderers, rapists, thieves... So what else is new?

Just be strong, sisters. Never mind the names they'll call us, their pathetic pleas and hard-luck stories, the physical and

---

5 Modern (1950).

emotional blackmail, the sure-thing investment opportunities, and all the other forms of backlash that will inevitably ensue once men realise they're broke. Just be brave and take the moolah.

It is only a matter of waiting it out. Once worldwide matriarchy is firmly established, women will at last be adequately safeguarded against male petulance. (Just being safeguarded against male *decor* decisions would be progress.)

So, TAKE THE MONEY HONEY, and take it proudly. You've nothing to lose but your chains and your poverty and your crappy job and your crap pension and your unheard voice and your unpaid domestic labour and your painful stilettos and your time-consuming beauty treatments, and about a million trillion mother-in-law jokes.

Just TAKE THE MONEY. It's not prostitution, it's your civic duty. Your *skivvy* duty. Take it for Carmen's sake, take it for all the opera divas who died in poverty, take it for the maids of all work, take it for all the women violated and unavenged, take it for the seven brides of seven brothers and that woman still stuck in her wedding dress. Take it for the powerless and penniless — so that someday you can empower them.

Take it for your *mother*, take it for your *daughter*. Come on. Just take it. Take the money and run! Take men for a ride, take them to the cleaners! Take the house, take the kids, take the cake!

And for godsake take the Pill while you're at it, or something equivalent. Let's face it, motherhood is for the birds. If it weren't for hormones, instinct, propaganda, peer pressure, tax cuts, faulty contraceptives, and an idle hankering to reread old children's books, nobody would ever procreate.[6]

---

6 As Audre Lorde wrote, 'Only within a patriarchal structure is maternity the only social power open to women' (*The Master's Tools Will Never Dismantle the Master's House*, Penguin, 2017).

SOURCES

Things Are Against Us
Previously unpublished.

The Underground Bunker
First published in the *Irish Times*, July 8, 2019, under the title 'Did we really massacre Indians, enslave Africans and poison rivers for this hellhole?'.

Trapped Family Fingers
First published in *The Globe & Mail*, October 12, 2019, under the title 'It's a mad, mad, mad, mad country'.

Three Strikes
First published in *The Baffler*, March 2015.

A Spell of Patriarchy
First published in the *New York Times*, December 26, 2019, under the title 'Patriarchy Is Just a Spell'.

Third-Rate Zeros
Previously unpublished.

Consider Pistons and Pumps
First published in *The Baffler*, September 5, 2016, under the title 'Womb Up, America!'.

The Woman of the House
First published in *The Guardian*, December 28, 2012, under the title 'The Little House books as feminist classics'.

The Lost Art of Staying Put
First published in *The Baffler*, December 2017.

Bras: a Life Sentence
First published in *Deliberately Thirsty*, ed. Sean Bradley, Argyll Publishing, August 2000.

Morning Routine Girls
First published in *The Baffler*, October 2015, under the title 'Distressed Cut-Offs: The morning angst'.

Sing the Unelectric
First published in *Aeon Magazine*, January 24, 2013, under the title 'Sing the Body Unelectric'.

Ah, Men
Previously unpublished.

Take the Money Honey
First published in *The Evergreen: A New Season in the North*, Volume IV, ed. Lucy Ellmann, The Word Bank, 2019; based on a talk given at the Poisson Rouge, New York, March 18, 2015.

꙰

Many thanks to commissioning editors Mark Medley, Martin Doyle, Valerie Cortes, Chris Lehmann, John Summers, Peter Catapano, Justine Jordan, Sean Bradley, and Marina Benjamin. It's nice to be asked.

ABOUT THE AUTHOR

Here's the THING: Lucy Ellmann is extremely shy. She's so awkward and self-conscious that meeting strangers, or almost anyone, exhausts her. She's lousy at remembering names. She cannot add or subtract. She hates having appointments in her diary and prefers to wear the same outfit every day. She's a fretful iconoclast, much prone to anger. She's also distrustful, lazy and easily hurt. She is not a team player. She prefers interrupting people to organising them, and cries if she doesn't get her way. She fears she's neglected everybody she knows, and vice versa – not to mention people she doesn't know. She can't stand protocol, committees, business hours, ceremonial occasions, public performances and filling out forms. And she never wants to be carried through a crowd on a palanquin. Otherwise, the world's her oyster!

She has written seven novels, including *Sweet Desserts* (Guardian Fiction Prize, 1988), *Dot in the Universe*, *Mimi* and *Ducks, Newburyport* (Goldsmiths Prize, James Tait Black Memorial Prize, 2019), and an illustrated book for adults, called *Tom the Obscure*. Born in the USA, she now lives in Scotland. This is her first book of essays.

NB. If this book results in one extra multiple orgasm some-where, aided by a repentant man who's finally seen where his true responsibilities lie, my work here is done. The hills should be alive with the sounds of ecstasy.

GALLEY BEGGAR PRESS

We hope that you've enjoyed *Things Are Against Us*. If you would like to find out more about Lucy, along with some of her fellow authors, head to www.galleybeggar.co.uk.

There, you will also find information about our subscription scheme, 'Galley Buddies', which is there to ensure we can continue to put out ambitious and unusual books like *Things Are Against Us*.

Subscribers to Galley Beggar Press:

· Receive limited black cover editions of our future titles (printed in a one-time run of 500).

· Have their names included in a special acknowledgement section at the back of our books.

· Are sent regular updates and invitations to our book launches, talks and other events.

· Enjoy a 20% discount code for the purchase of any of our backlist (as well as for general use throughout our online shop).

WHY BE A GALLEY BUDDY?

At Galley Beggar Press we don't want to compromise on the excellence of the writing we put out, or the physical quality of our books. We've also enjoyed numerous successes and prize nominations since we set up, in 2012. Almost all of our authors have gone on to be longlisted, shortlisted, or the winners of over twenty of the world's most prestigious literary awards.

But publishing for the sake of art is a risky commercial strategy. In order to keep putting out the very best books we can, and to continue to support talented writers, we need your help. The money we receive from our Galley Buddy scheme is an essential part of keeping us going.

By becoming a Galley Buddy, you help us to launch and foster a new generation of writers.

To join today, head to:
https://www.galleybeggar.co.uk/subscribe

Galley Beggar Press would like to thank the following individuals, without the generous support of whom our books would not be possible:

Ann Abineri
Kémy Ade
Timothy Ahern
Andrew Ainscough
Sam Ainsworth
Jez Aitchison
Simon Andrup
Callum Akaas
Ayodeji Alaka
Joseph H Alexander
Carol Allen
Richard Allen
Lulu Allison
Barbaros Altug
Kirk Annett
Eleanor Anstruther
Ebba Aquila
Elizabeth Aquino
Deborah Arata
Darryl Ardle
Robert Armiger
Sheila Armstrong
Sean Arnold
Curt Arnson
Xanthe Ashburner
Bethany Ashley
Robert Ashton
Adrian Astur Alvarez
Edmund Atrill
Vaida Aviks
Jo Ayoubi
Kerim Aytac
Claire Back
Andrew Bailey
Dexter Bailey
Tom Bailey
Edward Baines
Dawn Baird
Stephen Baird
Glynis Baker
Andrea Barlien
Chad Barnes
Ian Bartlett
Phil Bartlett

Rachel Beale
James Beavis
Rachel Bedder
Joseph Bell
Angel Belsey
Felicity Bentham
Michelle Best
Gary Betts
David Bevan
Alison Bianchi
Benjamin Bird
Sandra Birnie
Peter Blackett
Matt Blackstock
Adam Blackwell
Melissa Blaschke
Lynne Blundell
David Boddy
Sophie Boden
John Bogg
Heleen Boons
Nicholas Bouskill
Poppy Boutell
Edwina Bowen
Michelle Bowles
Joanna Bowman
David Bradley
Sean Bradley
Andrew J. Bremner
Aisling Brennan
Joan Brennan
Amanda Bringans
Erin Britton
Julia Brocking
Ben Brooks
Dean Brooks
Lily Brown
Sheila Browse
Peter Brown
Carrie Brunt
Richard Bryant
Justine Budenz
Lesley Budge
Laura Bui

Tony Burke
Kevin Burrell
Alister Burton
Bryan Burton
Joyce Butler
Barbara Byar
Barry Byrne
Rebecca Café
Max Cairnduff
Alan Calder
June Caldwell
Lloyd Calegan
Christopher Caless
Alfric Campbell
Mark Campbell
Laura Canning
Joanna Cannon
Annette Capel
Rhian Capener
Thomas Carlisle
Leona Carpenter
Sean Carroll
Richard Carter
Shaun Carter
Stuart Carter
Soraya Cary
Liam Casey
Leigh Chambers
David Charles
Richard Chatterton
Marcus Cheetham
Rose Chernick
Lina Christopoulou
Neal Chuang
Neil Churchill
Enrico Cioni
Douglas Clarke-Williams
Steve Clough
Paul Cole
Faith Coles
Jennifer Coles
John Coles
Emma Coley
Sam Coley

Tonia Collett
Gordon Collins
Gerard Connors
Helene Conrady
Joe Cooney
Kenneth Cooper
Sarah Corbett
Paul Corry
Andy Corsham
Mary Costello
Sally Cott
Nick Coupe
Andrew Cowan
Diarmuid Cowan
Felicity Cowie
Isabelle Coy-Dibley
Matthew Craig
Nick Craske
Anne Craven
Emma Crawford
Anne-Marie Creamer
Alan Crilly
Joanna Crispin
Ian Critchley
Brenda Croskery
James Cross
Kate Crowcroft
Miles Crowley
Stephen Cuckney
Damian Cummings
Stephen Cummins
Andrew Cupples
HC
Emma Curtis Lake
Chris Cusack
Siddharth Dalal
Elisa Damiani
Rachel Darling
Rupert Dastur
Claudia Daventry
Mark Davidson
Harriet Davies
Jessica Davies
Julie Davies
Linda Davies
Nickey Davies
Paul Davies
Alice Davis
Joshua Davis
Toby Day
Robin Deitch
Rebecca Demaree
Stanislaus Dempsey
Paul Dettmann

Turner Docherty
William Dobson
Dennis Donathan
Kirsty Doole
Kelly Doonan
Oliver Dorostkar
David Douce
Janet Dowling
Kelly Downey
Jamie Downs
Guy Dryburgh-Smith
Ian Dudley
Fiona Duffy
Florian Duijsens
Anthony Duncan
Antony Dunford
Stanka Easton
David Edwards
Nicola Edwards
Lance Ehrman
Jonathan Elkon
Ben Ellison
Ian Ellison
Thomas Ellmer
Stefan Erhardt
Alice Erskine
Fiona Erskine
Simeon Esper
Paul Ewen
Adam Fales
Monique Fare
Sarah Farley
Lori Feathers
Gerard Feehily
Jeremy Felt
Timothy Fenech
Vitcoria Fendall
Michael Fenton
Charles Fernyhough
Edward J. Field
Paul Fielder
Joy Finlayson
Elizabeth Finn
Catriona Firth
Becky Fisher
Fitzcarraldo Editions
Holly Fitzgerald
Eleanor Fitzsimons
Alexander Fleming
Grace Fletcher-Hackwood
Hayley Flockhart
Nicholas Flower
Patrick Foley
James Fourniere

Ceriel Fousert
Richard Fradgley
Pauline France
Matthew Francis
Frank Francisconi
Emily Fraser
Annette Freeman
Emma French
Ruth Frendo
Melissa Fu
Graham Fulcher
Paul Fulcher
Lew Furber
Stephen Furlong
Michael Furness
Brid Gallagher
Timothy Gallimore
Marc Galvin
Annabel Gaskell
Honor Gavin
Michael Geisser
Phil Gibby
Alison Gibson
Nolan Geoghegan
Neil George
Andy Godber
James Goddard
Stephanie Golding
Elizabeth Goldman
Morgan Golf-French
Matthew Goodman
Sakura Gooneratne
Sara Gore
Nikheel Gorolay
Cathy Goudie
Simon Goudie
Emily Grabham
Paul Greaves
Louise Greenberg
Chris Gribble
Judith Griffith
Neil Griffiths
Ben Griffiths
Vicki Grimshaw
Sam Guglani
Robbie Guillory
Dave Gunning
David Gunning
Andrew Gummerson
Rhys Gwyther
Ian Hagues
Daniel Hahn
Alice Halliday
Peter Halliwell

Karen Hamilton
Emma Hammond
Paul Handley
Rachel Handley
Kirsteen Hardie
Hal Harding-Jones
Vanessa Harris
Jill Harrison
Alice Harvey
Becky Harvey
Shelley Hastings
Simon Hawkesworth
Sarah Hawthorn
Patricia Hayes
David Hebblethwaite
Richard Hemmings
Padraig J. Heneghan
Stu Hennigan
Penelope Hewett Brown
Felix Hewison-Carter
Martin Hickman
Alexander Highfield
Jennifer Hill
Molly Hill
Susan Hill
Daniel Hillman
Rod Hines
Ned Hirst
Alex Hitch
Marcus Hobson
Peter Hodgkinson
Camilla Hoel
Aisling Holling
Tim Hopkins
Shane Horgan
Rashad Hosein
William Hsieh
Hugh Hudson
Anna Jean Hughes
Emily Hughes
Gavin Hughes
Richard Hughes
Robert Hughes
Andy Hunt
Kim-ling Humphrey
Louise Hussey
LJ Hutchins
Simone Hutchinson
Simon Issatt
Joseph Jackson
Paul Jackson
Jane Jakeman
Hayley James
Gareth Jelley

Kavita A. Jindal
Alice Jolly
George Johnson
Jane Johnson
Bevan Jones
Emma Jones
Jupiter Jones
Kerry-Louise Jones
Rebecca Jones
Amy Jordison
Anna Jordison
Diana Jordison
Atul Joshi
Claire Jost
Benjamin Judge
Gary Kaill
Darren Kane
Laura Kaye
Thomas Kealy
Andrew Kelly
Michael Ketchum
Peter Kettle
Jeffrey Kichen
Vijay Khurana
Jacqueline Knott
Amy Koheealiee
Teddy Kristiansen
Elisabeth Kumar
Gage LaFleur
Philip Lane
Domonique Lane-
  Osherov
I Lang
Kathy Lanzarotti
Jackie Law
Jo Lawrence
Sue Lawson
Rick Le Coyte
Carley Lee
Liz and Pete Lee
Darren Lerigo
Joyce Lillie Robinson
Yin Lim
Rebecca Lake
Rachel Lalchan
Eric Langley
Catherine Latsis
Elizabeth Leach
Ferdia Lennon
Joanne Leonard
Chiara Levorato
Mark Lewis
Elizabeth Leyland
Christian Livermore

Jesse Loncraine
Katie Long
Nick Lord Lancaster
Isaac Lowe
Lele Lucas
Sean Lusk
Simona Lyons
Marc Lyth
Jean Mackay
Wendy and Dave MacKay
Victoria MacKenzie
Tom MacLean
Andrea Macleod
Duncan Mackie
Brendan Madden
Joseph Maffey
Anne Maguire
Eleanor Maier
Johnny Mains
Philip Makatrewicz
Anil Malhotra
Tom Mandall
Joshua Mandel
Matthew Mansell
Emily Marchant
Chiara Margiotta
John Marr
Natalie Marshall
Paul Marshall
Iain Martin
Amanda Mason
Rosalind May
Philip Maynard
Stephen Maynard
Sally Mayor
Sara McCallum
Amy McCauley
Paul McCombs
Ella McCrystle
Fabia McDougall
Kieran McGrath
Sheila McIntosh
Alan McIntyre
Gerald McWilliams
Victor Meadowcraft
Jason Merrells
Andy Merrills
Tina Meyer
Ali Millar
Jacob Millard
Michael Millington
Phillipa Mills
Sally Minogue
Fiona Mitchell

Lotte Mitchell Reford
Ian Mond
Fiona Mongredien
Sue Mongredien
Alexander Monker
Alex Moore
Clare Moore
Gary Moore
Michelle Moorhouse
Rachael de Moravia
Nigel J. Morgan
Carlos Eduardo Morreo
Jackie Morris
Julie Morris
Patrick Morris
Clive Morrison
Donald Morrison
Roger Morrison
David Musgrave
Electra Nanou
Polly Nash
Zosha Nash
Linda Nathan
Tim Neighbour
Amanda Nicholls
Catherine Nicholson
Sophia Nixon
Mariah de Nor
Calum Novak-Mitchell
Anna Nsubuga
Georgina Nugent-Folan
Arif Nurmohamed
James O'Brien
Liam and Wendy
    O'Connor
Rodney O'Connor
Richard Offer
Seb Ohsan-Berthelsen
Janet Oliver
Alec Olsen
Laura Oosterbeek
Sheila O'Reilly
Valerie O'Riordan
Liz O'Sullivan
Jack Oxford
Jenny Owen
Steven Palter
Dave Parry
Gary Partington
Debra Patek
Nicholas Paton Philip
Ian Patterson
Nigel Paulson
Stephen Pearsall

Alexa Pearson
Rebecca Peer
Jonathan Perks
Connor Perrie
Tom Perrin
Tony Pettigrew
Dan Phillips
Jennifer Pink
Robert Pisani
Ben Plouviez
Louise Pointer
Erin Polmear
James Pomar
Jonathan Pool
Giacomo Pope
Christopher Potter
Ailsa Power
Trine Prescott
Lesley Preston
David Primost
David Prince
Victoria Proctor
Jill Propst
Samuel Pryce
James Puddephatt
Joyce Pugh
Alan Pulverness
Sarah Pybus
Richard Pye
Alex Pykett
Lisa Quattromini
Leng Leng Quek
Shiva Rahbaran
Sim Ralph
Polly Randall
Jane Rawson
Euan Reed
Dawn Rees
Padraig Reidy
Emma Reitano
Barbara Renel
Vasco Resende
Amy Reynolds
Gaynor Reynolds
Annie Rhodes
Alison Riley
Thea Marie Rishovd
Laura Roach
Chris Roberts
Stephen Roberts
Rocky and Kat
Liz Roe
Brian Ronan
Angela Rose

Kalina Rose
Wendy Ross
Nathan Rowley
Martin Rowsell
Beverly Rudy
Giles Ruffer
Libby Ruffle
Tomilyn Rupert
Tim Russ
Rebeka Russell
Naben Ruthnum
John Rutter
Tobias Ryan
Amanda Saint
Floriane Sajdak
Alison Sakai
Michael Saler
Himanshu Kamal Saliya
Robert Sanderson
Valentina Santolini
Lior Sayada
Liam Scallon
Amy Scarrott
Linde Schaafsma
Robert Scheffel
Jordan Schlipf
Benedict Schofield
Florian Schroiff
Jan Schoones
Ros Schwartz
Nicola Scott
Stephen Robert Scott
James Scudamore
Miss Scullion
Darren Seeley
Kelly Selby-Jones
Elie Sharp
Samuel Sharps
Richard Sheehan
Nicola Shepherd
Emma Shore
Larry Sides
Deborah Siddoway
Kate Simpson
Yvonne Singh
Ann Slack
Jay Slayton-Joslin
Ben Smith
Chris Smith
Connor Smith
Hazel Smith
Ian Smith
Kieron Smith
Nicola Smith

Shannon Smith
Tom Smyth
Lisa Solley
Louise Soraya Black
Arabella Spencer
Karmen Spiljak
Sarah Spitz
Hannah Spruce
Chiara Spruijt
Connor Stait
Karl Stange
Daniel Staniforth
Cathryn Steele
Gillian Stern
Stewart Stevens
Mark Stevenson
Tabatha Stirling
Dagmara Stoic
Justina Stonyte
Anne Storr
Colette Storrow
Elizabeth Stott
Jochen Stremmel
Julia Stringwell
Andrew Stuart
Zara Stubbs
Daryl Sullivan
Jesse Surridge
Drashti Sutariya
Juliet Sutcliffe
Helen Swain
Helen Symington
Ewan Tant
Sarah Tapp
Justine Taylor
Peter Talor
Moray Teale
Alan Teder
Gill Thackray
Vivienne Thackray
Natalia Theodoridou
Cennin Thomas

Sue Thomas
Susannah Thompson
Caroline Thomson
Graham Thornelow
Sam Thorp
Nan Tilghman
Matthew Tilt
Amie Tolson
Margaret Tongue
James Torrence
Kate Triggs
Steve Tuffnell
Devin Tupper
Nick Turner
Harriet Tyce
Eleanor Updegraff
Raminta Uselyte
Esther Van Buul
Bart Van Overmeire
Nicole Vanderbilt
David Varley
Francesca Veneziano
Irene Verdiesen
Essi Viding
Boris Vidovic
Bea Vincent
Meg Vincent
Gabriel Vogt
Stephen Waderman
Julia Wait
Chris Walker
Phoebe Walker
Stephen Walker
Ben Waller
MJ Wallis
Sinead Walsh
Steve Walsh
David Ward
Jerry Ward
Kate Ward
Peter Ward
Rachael Wardell

Guy Ware
Emma Warnock
Ellie Warren
Stephanie Wasek
Daniel Waterfield
Sarah Webb
Lucy Webster
Adam Welch
Clemency Wells
Nathan Wescott
Karl Ruben Weseth
Jo West-Moore
Mark Wharton
Tom Whatmore
Wendy Whidden
Robert White
Indra Wignall
Kyra Wilder
Claire Willerton
G Williams
Sam Williams
Sharon Williams
Courtney Williamson
Sarah Wiltshire
Kyle Winkler
Bianca Winter
Lucie Winter
Sheena Winter
Simon Winter
Astrid Maria Wissenburg
Stephen Witkowski
Jonathan Wood
Nathan Wood
Paul Woodgate
Emma Woolerton
Christine Wyse
Ben Yeoh
Ian Young
Juliano Zaffino
Sylvie Zannier
Rupert Ziziros
Carsten Zwaaneveld